# Old
# Carrick

Maidens, looking northwards along the rough uneven track of the Shore Road. Directly ahead is Ardlochan and the trees of Culzean Estate. This view from the 1940s has since changed considerably with the building of many detached villas on the landward side of the road.

...was ...s run by ...his wife Margaret, ...ed in a corner of their ...chen in a small single-storey thatched cottage near the end of the Monkwood Mains Road. Following his death in 1872, Margaret continued to run the post office until 17 February 1910, when she passed away at the age of 94 years and 10 months. She was the oldest postmistress in Great Britain at the time of her death and is pictured here standing outside her home and post office. In the window is the letterbox and a number of postcards for sale depicting local views of the village. The row of cottages was later demolished but Minishant still has its own little post office which is now ...ed next to the old red telephone ...d the Minishant Inn.

...ugh Maxwell
...ed in the United
...dom, 2010
...blishing Limited
...e, Catrine, KA5 6RD
...enlake.co.uk

...781840335095

## Acknowledgements

I would like to acknowledge the invaluable help of the many people living within the towns and villages of South Ayrshire who contributed information towards the book. I would also like to thank the staffs of the reference department at the Dick Institute, Kilmarnock, and also the local history department of the Carnegie Library, Ayr.

## Further Reading

The Statistical Account of Scotland, 1791–1799.
The New Statistical Account of Scotland, 1845.
The Third Statistical Account of Scotland, 1951.
Ken Andrew, Guide to the Kyle and Carrick District of Ayrshire, 1981.
Rev. R. Lawson, Places of Interest about Maybole, 1891.
Rev. R. Lawson, Places of Interest about Girvan, 1892.
Rev. R. Lawson, Views of Carrick, 1894.
Dane Love, Ayrshire – Discovering a County, 2003.

James MacKenna, Round about Girvan, 1906.
J. Kevan McDowall, Carrick Gallovidian, 1947.
Rotary Club of Girvan, Girvan 1668–1968 (300th Anniversary booklet), 1968.
John Strawthorn, Ayrshire – The Story of a County, 1975.
www.maybole.org – an excellent source of information on Maybole and South Ayrshire.

# Introduction

The district of Carrick in South Ayrshire is bounded to the north by the winding course of the River Doon, to the east by Loch Doon, to the south by the remote moorland hills of Galloway and to the west by the waters of the Firth of Clyde. The word Carrick is corrupted from the Gaelic word 'carraig', meaning a rock or a rocky place, and this is an apt description when one considers the miles of exposed rocky cliffs and shoreline along its coastal fringes.

This area was originally part of the Kingdom of Galloway and was ruled over by its lords until 1186 when it was granted to Duncan, son of Gilbert of Galloway, who became the first Earl of Carrick. While residing at Turnberry Castle he founded Crossraguel Abbey, possibly as a thanksgiving for this title. His son Neil became the second Earl of Carrick but he had no male heir so his daughter Margaret inherited the title to become the Countess of Carrick.

Margaret married Adam de Kilconquhar who became the third Earl of Carrick, but he was killed in Palestine in 1270. She married Robert Bruce, the Lord of Annandale and Cleveland, and on 11 June 1274 gave birth at Turnberry Castle to a son, also named Robert.

Robert was only eighteen when his mother died in 1292 and the Earldom of Carrick fell to him. Four years later, along with his father, he swore fealty to Edward at Berwick but rescinded this the following year, beginning the long struggle for Scottish independence. He was crowned King of Scotland at Scone in 1306 and his guerrilla campaign against the English eventually culminated in victory at the Battle of Bannockburn in 1314.

Carrick saw some involvement with the wars of independence, and was again rife with conflict throughout the sixteenth and seventeenth centuries as the district's powerful landowning families openly engaged in bitter and deadly feuds with each other over land, property and honour. The Kennedys were the most powerful and influential family in Carrick at this time and they had numerous castles and keeps dotted along the coastline and located inland near settlements or overlooking principal routes. The Cassillis and Bargany branches of the Kennedy family even resorted to open murder; Gilbert Kennedy, the last of the great Ardstinchar and Bargany lairds, was murdered at the age of 25 at Maybole in 1601, in a fight with his cousin, the Earl of Cassillis. His tomb can be found in the old graveyard at Ballantrae.

With its scattered villages the district was also sufficiently rugged and secluded to become a favourite haunt of those persecuted during the Covenanting times of the seventeenth century, and martyrs' tombstones and monuments exist at Maybole, Straiton, Colmonell, Barrhill, Kirkmichael, Old Dailly and at Barr.

By the end of the 1600s Carrick was divided into nine separate parishes, with Maybole becoming the capital town as it was the provincial seat of the Earls of Cassillis. The parish of Dailly was unique in that it was the only inland parish within Scotland to have an island within its boundaries in the form of Ailsa Craig.

From the 1750s many of the influential and wealthy local families turned their attention to improving their estates and important agricultural improvements began to be

Craigneil Castle, near Colmonell, was reputed to have been built during the thirteenth century by Neil, Earl of Carrick, hence its designation as Craigneil, but most of it appears to date from the fifteenth century. In the sixteenth century it became the occasional residence of John, fifth Earl of Cassillis, and, at all times, the halfway or halting place of the family and their retinue when travelling between Cassillis and Castle Kennedy, their principal stronghold in Galloway. In 1886, one side of the tower collapsed into a stone quarry that was being worked below it.

implemented throughout the district. The early pioneers were Sir Adam Fergusson of Kilkerran, David, tenth Earl of Cassillis at Culzean, Thomas Kennedy of Dunure, and Lt Col. Sir Andrew Cathcart of Carleton. Land was drained and enclosed, with lime and manure being used to improve the quality of the soil for crops and livestock. Extensive woodlands were also cut down to clear the land for farming and to supply the nearby towns and the rest of Ayrshire with the raw material for building and for fuel.

Fishing was another industry that had been carried out along the coast since ancient times and commercial fisheries existed at Dunure, Maidens, Ballantrae and Girvan which became Carrick's principal seaport. The Firth of Clyde and surrounding waters were abundant in cod, haddock and many other types of white fish, while salmon were netted commercially at the mouths of the River Stinchar and the Water of Girvan.

The rugged Carrick coastline with its many hidden bays and rocky coves was ideally suited to the practice of smuggling which was carried out actively by those who lived in the towns and villages along the coast. Ballantrae was frequently described as a noted haunt of smugglers, with French luggers perpetually hovering off the coast with their cargos of brandy

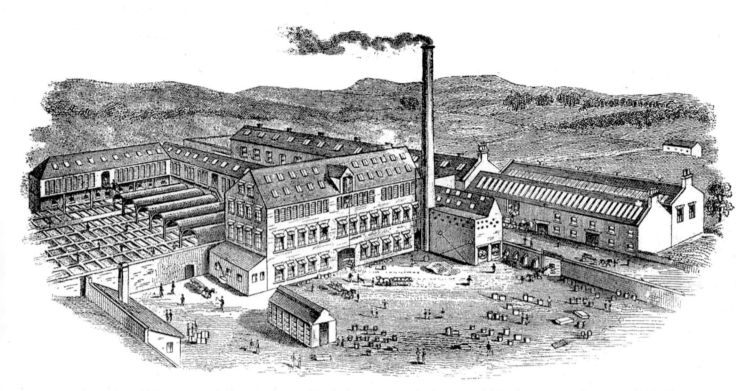

**The Ladywell Tannery and Shoe Factory at Maybole was once the largest within the town and was established around 1870 by John Gray and Co. At its heyday in 1890 over 400 men and women were employed by the works and they produced 5,000 pairs of shoes and boots a week. The company also owned a retail chain of over 60 shops in many of the towns and cities across Britain. A slump in the boot and shoe industry saw production decline at the works and the workforce was also reduced with the factory closing in 1907. The tannery was later purchased by the Miller Tanning Co. Ltd, and employed about 40 or so men who continued to produce sole leathers until May 1969 when it also closed.**

and fine linens. Further inland, contraband goods were also being brought on packhorse and cart over the wild moors from Galloway into Ayrshire and then beyond to Glasgow.

Handloom weaving became a significant industry and the click-clack of the loom could be heard at all hours of the day in nearly every town and village. It led directly to the establishment of communities at Kirkmichael and Crosshill and also brought much needed prosperity to the larger towns of Maybole and Girvan, where, by the 1840s, over 2,000 looms were in production. The manufacture of cotton and the comfortable living it provided saw many immigrants from Ireland travel over to find work and settle with their families in south Ayrshire.

The trade prospered until the introduction of the power loom towards the end of the nineteenth century led to a steady decline in trade. Many families had to move outwith the district to the larger mills at Kilmarnock, Glasgow and in the Irvine Valley and as a result the population declined, although some travelled to Maybole to find work within the boot and shoe trade. Following the decline of handloom weaving, this and some coal mining near Dailly were the only industries left within Carrick.

By 1891 Maybole had ten shoe factories in full production, employing over 1,500 workers who produced about one million pairs of leather boots and shoes annually. A chain of shops known as the 'Maybole Shoe Shop' or the 'Maybole Boot Co.' had also been created, with stores throughout Britain.

This trade flourished until 1907 when the largest factory in Maybole at Ladywell closed. The works were the largest employer within the town and as the trade continued to decline and other factories closed, many families emigrated overseas to Canada. Despite slight upsurges in demand for leather footwear during both world wars, by 1970 all the factories had closed down in Maybole.

The railway reached Carrick in 1857 when the line was extended from Ayr to Maybole and thence to Girvan in 1860, reaching Stranraer sixteen years later. Thousands of people flocked to the coast and the coastal town of Girvan during the Glasgow Summer Fair and all manner of entertainments and shows were held to attract visitors. Regular horsedrawn coach tours also departed from Girvan, travelling down the coast to Ballantrae, then inland to Colmonell and back via Pinwherry and Pinmore, allowing many visitors to explore the scenic charms of the surrounding district. Carrick had much to entice the visitor with its fine links courses at Turnberry, rivers for fishing, beautiful wooded valleys, a magnificent coastline with sandy beaches and fine views, and as a result many of the small villages along the coast such as Dunure, Lendalfoot and Maidens also expanded to cater for this annual influx of holidaymakers.

The fertile sandy soil near the coast is also well suited to the growing of early potatoes and from the 1850s Ayrshire gained a reputation as the potatoes were not only the earliest on the market in Scotland but also high in quality and taste. Popular varieties included Epicure, Redbogs, Goodrich, Dons, Jubilee and Puritan. The terrain inland was much less fertile, more undulating and hilly and was therefore more suited to the grazing of livestock such as sheep and cattle.

Coal was also worked to a considerable extent on many of the estates within the Girvan Valley surrounding Dailly, and over 110 mines are known to have existed. It is recorded that the monks of Crossraguel Abbey first worked coal from surface outcrops in 1405. Hundreds of men worked down the pits but the last mine at Dalquharran near Dailly closed in 1977, bringing to an end the legacy of coal mining within the district.

In recent years much of the rough hilly land surrounding the inland villages of Straiton, Barr and Barrhill has been commercially planted with conifers and this has brought a new industry to the district in the form of forestry management.

Almost all the Carrick fishing fleets have now disappeared due to decreasing fish numbers, increasing cost and the introduction of quotas. Many harbours are now only frequented by small pleasure craft and at Girvan the few surviving fishing boats are now outnumbered in the harbour by modern pleasure yachts.

Girvan, like the other coastal villages, declined as a holiday resort in the early 1960s when people began to travel abroad but in common with many other places it still welcomes a large influx of day trippers who flock to the coast by car on fine summer days. The once remote moorland villages also now receive frequent visitors as people escape from the congested towns and cities to explore the countryside. Many of the upland areas which were planted commercially with conifer forest are now easily accessible through construction of a network of paths and signs.

The Ayrshire Coastal Path has also now been created and this runs the length of the Carrick coastline from its start in Glen App to Ballantrae and then to Girvan and onwards to Dunure and Greenan, finally culminating in north Ayrshire at Skelmorlie.

Carrick has other attractions for visitors. Culzean Castle, one of the finest castles on the Scottish coast, attracts over 200,000 people every year. The Open Golf Championship is also regularly held at Turnberry and thousands of people from around the world descend on the challenging links courses to watch famous sportsmen compete for the Claret Jug. Carrick's historic towns and villages have retained much of their charm and character and the area remains synonymous with beautiful scenery and a proud and cherished history.

In 1938 the burgh council, in collaboration with the artist James Wright, extensively landscaped the bare grassy area of shoreland south of the harbour of Girvan into a magnificent pleasure ground. The aim was to provide more amenities and attractions for day trippers and holidaymakers and this area became the focal point for all entertainments within the town, with outdoor fun being provided by the large boating lake, bathing station, children's yacht pond, shore gymnasium and putting greens. The Pleasure House with its shows and dances catered for the indoor fun at night. A large promenade was also constructed along the beach front with two fine ranges of comfortable bathing boxes, one section being reserved for the ladies and the other for the men, as well as toilets and changing facilities. The promenade was also attractively lit at night. This photograph from the late 1940s is looking north along the promenade towards the pier with the putting greens and boating lake visible on the right and the Pleasure House in the background adjacent the harbour.

Dunure dates from the early 1800s when many of the cottages were built and the place was advertised as being a favourable location for fishing and the export of coal could be carried out. An edition of the *Kilmarnock Standard* from March 1923 described the village thus: 'It is pleasant to watch the boats come sailing in, or to see the fishermen hanging out the nets to dry, the women gossiping cheerily at their doors, with the children playing at their feet. On the plateau in front of the ancient keep the younger fishermen in their blue jerseys play at football when their work for the time is done. The village lies in a deep, sheltered hollow, but on the height above there are a few cottages of modern construction. In these days of housing shortage there could be no more desirable place (in fine weather) for camping out than Dunure.' This photograph was taken from the rocks near Dunure Castle; towards the far left is the Kennedy Hall, built in 1881.

With a commanding position high up on a cliff overlooking the Firth of Clyde, Dunure Castle was once the principal stronghold in Carrick of the Kennedy family. The ruins date from the fourteenth century but it is commonly believed that a fort existed on the site prior to this and was attacked and captured by the Vikings under the command of King Haco of Norway in 1263. In August 1563 Mary, Queen of Scots, was a guest of the fourth Earl of Cassillis, Gilbert Kennedy, at the castle while she was touring southwest Scotland. In 1570 this same Gilbert roasted the Commendator of Crossraguel Abbey, Allan Stewart, over an open fire within the castle vault in an attempt to force him to sign away the valuable lands owned by the Abbey. The Commendator was badly burned and did indeed sign, but when he was later freed from the vault by rescuers and carried to the Cross in Ayr, he revoked his own signature and complained to the Privy Council although no further action was taken against the Earl of Cassillis. The fifteenth-century doocot is on the right of the photograph, while in the foreground is the putting green that forms part of the Kennedy Park, which was donated to the village in 1922 by Colonel Kennedy.

Nestled right on the shore just north of the harbour, Dunure House dates from the early nineteenth century with later additions. Dunure is surrounded by extensive shingle beaches both to the north and south of the harbour and some of the finest agate specimens in Ayrshire can be found on them. To the untrained eye these 'gemstones' are very difficult to spot as they have been weathered and smoothed on the outside and often look like any other common beach pebble. When cut open, however, the agates reveal beautiful and spectacular patterns in pink, blue, brown and cream.

The Dunure & Maidens Light Railway was constructed by the Glasgow & South Western Railway Company to transport passengers to the company's luxury hotel at Turnberry. Dunure Station opened on 17 May 1906 and was located about a mile to the northeast of the village. This is the view from the main road and on the right, overlooking the single-track line, is the wooden shed in the small goods yard. The line closed permanently to passenger services on 1 June 1933, but remained open for carrying freight in the form of early potatoes that were grown in the fields along the coast. These trains ran until the closure of the line in the mid 1950s and were known as the 'Potato Specials'. Today, the station is overgrown with trees and bushes and luxury villas occupy the site of the goods yard, which is now known as Fisherton Avenue.

After Dunure, the next station south on the light railway was at Knoweside. Visible in this photograph is the railway track and small platform, while just out of view was a level crossing over the road that led down to the sandy beach at Croy. On the left the wooden struts of the large water tank are also visible; whenever a train stopped to fill up with water it sat directly on the level crossing, temporarily blocking the road to all traffic. A small goods yard and loop were also constructed at Knoweside. Just to the north of the station site is the famous Croy Electric Brae.

Built from golden sandstone in the Gothic-style by Robert Adam in the years 1777–92, Culzean is one of the finest castles in Scotland. An old tower house had occupied the rocky clifftop site since the twelfth century and Adam, working under the direction of David Kennedy, tenth Earl of Cassillis, incorporated the older Kennedy fort within the new building. An oval staircase dominates the interior of the castle, which also contains an extensive armoury, a number of large drawing and dining rooms, a library and sitting room, and also several lavish and comfortable dressing rooms, bedrooms or apartments, many with magnificent views over the Firth of Clyde. A west wing, housing a number of apartments, was added in the years 1875–78 and is visible in this photograph. Culzean Castle passed to the National Trust for Scotland in 1945 and at this time the top flat in the west wing was transformed into the Eisenhower Apartment for use by General Dwight D. Eisenhower, Supreme Commander of Allied forces during the liberation of Europe. This was a gift from the Scottish people and he stayed at the castle four times, once while he was President of the United States.

A large fountain and pond surrounded by a lawn form the centrepiece of the castle gardens at Culzean. Known as the 'Fountain Court', it is reached by walking along ivy-clad castellated terraces planted with all manner of native and exotic plants and climbers. In his book, *Views of Carrick* (1894), the Rev. R. Lawson describes Culzean Castle as being 'the most palatial edifice in the locality, and yet by reason of the height of the cliff on which it stands (100 feet) the building itself looks inconspicuous. It was built in 1777, the previous house being called Cove, taking its name from the remarkable caves which here penetrate the cliff. Through the kindness of Lord Ailsa, the grounds are open to visitors on Wednesdays, on application to Mr Smith, factor. Upwards of a thousand persons, annually, avail themselves of the privilege.' Today, visitors number around 200,000 annually. Visible in the background of this photograph is the clock tower which forms part of the Clock Tower courtyard. From here visitors can stand next to three large cannons, designed to defend the castle from sea attackers, and enjoy the tremendous sweeping views out across the Firth of Clyde to Arran.

Created in the early nineteenth century by flooding a large boggy meadow, 'The Pond' or 'Swan Pond' at Culzean covers roughly thirteen acres and is located within the south end of the estate. It is reached from the castle by walking along a pleasant woodland path and the waters were once stocked with trout, perch and ruddy for fishing by the first Marquis of Ailsa. Swans were also introduced and bred in large numbers and, as can be seen in this photograph from *c*.1907, many visitors enjoyed feeding them. In earlier times, the poor birds were pinioned to prevent them flying off as they would later become the main course in lavish banquets held within the castle. Culzean Castle and its estate of 563 acres were passed to the National Trust for Scotland in 1945 by the fifth Marquis of Ailsa. The estate became Scotland's first country park in 1969.

Last occupied by the MacIlvanes of Grimmet around 1800, the well-preserved ruins of Thomaston Castle are located adjacent to the main road near Culzean. A castle on the site was believed to have been built sometime in the thirteenth century by Thomas Bruce, nephew of Robert the Bruce, and this was extended during the sixteenth century with the addition of a square tower house. It had been owned by the Corries of Kelwood since 1507 but later passed through marriage to the MacIlvanes around 1632. The castle is L-shaped and was three storeys in height with a garret and corbelled-out parapet with the main entrance being located in the square tower. The basement or ground floor contained four chambers including the kitchen, wine cellar and access to the hall on the first floor. The upper floor would have contained the sleeping quarters for the residents.

This view of Maidens from around 1914 was taken from one of the large hillocks near the harbour known as the Knowes, and shows the sprawling nature of the village and the sweep of Maidenhead Bay. On the right is the Harbour Road where several wooden fishing boats have been drawn up onto the grass; further along, the main road from Ayr can be seen entering the village after several sharp turns. On the left is the row of cottages known as Seaview that later housed the post office, and which led to what was known as the Shore Road (now called Ardlochan Road). The village was once known as the Marquis Village after the Marquis of Ailsa who owned the land on which the first houses were built. It later became known as The Maidens, taking that name from the Maidenhead Rocks that lie just offshore near the entrance to the harbour.

Weary Neuk, next to Maidens harbour, is associated in legend with King Robert the Bruce. In 1306, after being crowned King of Scotland at Scone, Robert was forced into exile and became a fugitive hunted by the English. In the spring of 1307 he found himself on the island of Arran with some 300 men and a messenger was despatched across to the mainland to ascertain the strength of the English and to muster support for the king. When this had been done a fire was to be lit near the coast to let Robert know he could come over. Several weeks passed and eventually from the shores of Arran a fire was seen. Bruce and his men sailed across, coming ashore at the Weary Neuk area to discover that no fire had been lit and it was only whins burning on the hillside. Robert was heard to remark to his men when coming ashore at Maidens that the place was 'a weary neuk to land in'. Visible in this photograph from the early 1930s are the then recently built houses on the Harbour Road.

A local carrier on the main road from Ayr through Maidens. At the bottom of this stretch of road, where it turns sharply to the right, there is the Shanter Road which leads off to the left towards Shanter Farm. Near the modern farm there once stood an eighteenth-century steading, and it was while studying at Kirkoswald that Robert Burns and a friend went fishing at Maidens on a small boat called 'The Tam', belonging to Douglas Graham of Shanter. It proved to be an eventful fishing trip as the wind increased in strength and threatened to push the small vessel out into the open sea but the boys managed to reach the safety of the shore. The combination of names later provided the inspiration for one of Burns's most famous poems.

The smithy at Maidens was located along the Shore Road and is visible on the right of this photograph. On the left is the shoreline of the bay with the houses at Ardlochan. In the eighteenth century an old turnpike road went past the old mill at Ardlochan, over the Hogston Burn, and then through the policies of Culzean before descending again onto the shore at Culzean Bay. Today, this route has become popular with walkers on the Ayrshire Coastal Path and it is still possible to walk the old turnpike route into and through Culzean Estate.

The pier and harbour at Maidens date from the eighteenth century when many local people were employed in fishing for herring, cod and all other types of white fish. The mouth of the harbour was prone to silting up, making navigation nigh on impossible even for small vessels, so in the 1950s a completely new harbour pier and breakwater were constructed from the rubble left over following the demolition of the former RAF buildings and runways at nearby Turnberry. A long pier and breakwater were built on the west side incorporating some of the rocks that lay just offshore, while on the east side a narrow breakwater was also constructed. The busy harbour was again dredged to remove much of the silt and it was used frequently by a number of fishing vessels. However, by the early 1970s the mouth of the harbour had again become badly silted and boats were now forced to land their catches at Ayr and Girvan. This photograph from the early 1900s shows the old pier reaching out towards the Maidenhead Rocks in Maidenhead Bay. Today, the harbour is mainly used by small pleasure craft.

The 'Bathing Ground' at 'The Maidens', as the village is known by locals, was just south of the harbour at Port Murray where there was a small sandy beach bordered by a rocky shoreline. The remains of an old slipway exist here as several small steamboats were built in the early 1880s by the boat-building firm of Alexander MacCreadie, but in 1885 the yard (which was owned by the third Marquis of Ailsa) was transferred to Troon. Overlooking the bay today is the unique house called Port Murray, designed by Peter Womersley and built in 1960–63. Perched on the rocks, it is a long, low, glass and cedar wood construction that is often said to look almost gull-like in appearance when viewed from the sea.

Maidens Station on the Maidens & Dunure Light Railway was located to the east of the village. This is the view looking up the line that was 20 miles in length, running from the junction at Alloway down the Ayrshire coast to Girvan. The station had an island platform and a signal box, and also a small wooden building with overhanging canopies, which served as the ticket office and waiting room. The station was located to the south of the main road while the goods yard was on the opposite side of the road. The former goods yard has since become a caravan park.

At Souter Johnnie's House, Kirkoswald, Stone Figures —Tam o' Shanter, Souter Johnnie, and the Landlord and Landlady of Tam o' Shanter Inn, Ayr.

Souter Johnnie's House is located on Kirkoswald's Main Street. The single-storey, thatched-roof cottage was built in 1785 by John Davidson who was the village souter or shoemaker. Robert Burns became acquainted with him and his neighbour Douglas Graham while lodging near the village and attending school there in the summer of 1775. These two men, along with the other characters Burns met, became immortalised in his poem 'Tam O' Shanter'. Following Davidson's death in 1808 the cottage was divided into two separate dwellings and was later preserved by a local committee in the 1920s. The fictional characters from 'Tam O'Shanter' were sculpted from sandstone in the 1830s by James Thom and were exhibited and displayed across Britain before being acquired in 1924 for display at the cottage. As can be seen in this photograph, the life-size sculptures were originally placed within the garden but were later moved into a restored alehouse at the rear of the cottage to better protect them from the weather. Souter Johnnie's House is now preserved by the National Trust for Scotland.

Designed and built by James Millar for the Glasgow & South Western Railway Company, the Turnberry Hotel stands on a small plateau overlooking the links golf courses. It was officially opened on 17 May 1906. Inside it was very luxurious with electric lighting, central heating, hot and cold running water, saltwater plunge baths and 100 well-furnished bedrooms, many with excellent views out across the Firth of Clyde. On the opening day a special train, carrying the railway directors and their invited guests, ran on the light railway from Ayr to the hotel where a lavish lunch was served and a round of golf was enjoyed on the links courses. During the First World War the hotel was requisitioned for use by the Royal Flying Corps for training pilots and following the outbreak of the Second World War the hotel was again used, this time as a military hospital. In recent years a spa and leisure complex, an activity centre, luxury lodges and the Colin Montgomerie Links Academy have all been opened and the hotel also underwent a major refurbishment prior to hosting the 2009 Open Championship. On the right is the golf clubhouse.

After being requisitioned for use during both world wars the links courses at Turnberry were extensively restored and redesigned to mask the old concrete runways and the former air force buildings. The Ailsa Course has now become one of the most famous and challenging links courses in the world. It is a par 70, 7,211-yard course, and was named after the Marquis of Ailsa who once owned the land on which it is built. The course's first professional tournament was played in 1908. The Open Championship has also been held here four times with Tom Watson winning in 1977, Greg Norman in 1986, Nick Price in 1994 and Stewart Cink in 2009. This photograph from the early 1900s shows the clubhouse or 'golf house' as it was known; in 1993 a new much larger clubhouse was officially opened by Prince Andrew.

The Dunure & Maidens Light Railway had numerous steep gradients and tight bends and provided passengers with spectacular views of the Carrick coastline; however, it was not a great success and closed to passenger transport in 1930. It did reopen very briefly for passengers in 1932 but closed again the following year, although it continued to be used by goods trains transporting early potatoes from the coast to markets in Ayr, Girvan and further afield. The line closed in December 1968. This photograph shows the station at Turnberry and for the convenience of passengers it was connected to the hotel by a glass-covered walkway. Also visible above the platform is the chimney of the boilerhouse that was used to provide power for the hotel.

Pictured on the main road that passes in front of the Turnberry Hotel in the early 1930s is a Crossley Golden Saloon, which became known as the 'Super Six'. Crossley Motors were based in Manchester and produced high quality motors between 1904 and 1936. Described in journals and newspapers of the time as 'a refined roomy car with fine all-round performance', the Golden Saloon was powered by a 3198cc engine that produced 21hp. Reaching a top speed of 70mph, with 0–50mph taking a lengthy 25 seconds, it was not very frugal compared to modern cars, with typical fuel consumption being in the region of 15.5mpg. The car in this photograph cost approximately £575 and came equipped with sporty wire wheels while at the rear of the vehicle, next to the spare wheel, was a bracket that folded down to hold the large luggage trunk.

Girvan harbour was always a hive of activity, and more so in the summer when holidaymakers and day trippers flocked to the town. In this scene the small steamship *Lady Ailsa* can be seen docked at the harbourside while also visible are the wooden rowing boats (known locally as 'punts') that could be hired to go around the harbour and up the course of the river. The Pleasure House on the left was always the place to go in the evening for dancing and shows which were often provided by the renowned Hampson's Pierrots and Julian Ross's Girvan Entertainers. In the 1931 season Tommy Harvey was the stage manager, Mamie Harvey worked the box office and the entertainers themselves were Tom Irving, Alice Young, Jack Rowlands, Sheila Grant, Julian Ross, Dave Bruce, Gladys De Marr and Minnie and Anna Sanrena. One of the rides of the travelling shows that often came to the town is in the background and further along are the large wooden frames used by the fishermen for drying their nets. This photograph was taken from an attic room of one of the houses on Knockcushan Street.

Girvan harbour, pictured on 15 May 1913 with the lugger *Fairy Queen* dominating the view while in the foreground are the wooden smacks that were used to fish the surrounding waters. In September 1915 the *Ayr Advertiser* reported on an unfortunate accident in an article entitled 'Harbour Mishap': 'While engaged loading some bags of grain into the goods steamer *Loch Nell* at Girvan Harbour on Thursday, James Gillespie, labourer, residing at McConnell's Square, Girvan, was struck by a bag which was being hoisted off the quay and he was knocked over the edge of the pier onto the deck of the steamer, falling a distance of ten or twelve feet. Gillespie was rendered unconscious for a time, and was taken home in a cab. He was badly bruised all over, but no bones were broken.'

A large catch of cod is landed at the harbour side, fishermen standing ready with salt to cure the fish. According to the *Statistical Account of Scotland*, published in 1794, 'The bay of Girvan seems intended by nature as an excellent white-fishing station, and experience has proved that most of the best kinds such as cod, haddock, whiting, mackerel, sole, flounder, turbot, and lobster, are to be found in it. Strange to tell however, the taking of these fish has never been prosecuted with much energy. Nor have the Irish weavers, when unemployed and in a state of utter destitution, in consequence of a stagnation of trade, been at all in the habit of endeavouring to support their starving families with this easily acquired and excellent food. One spirited individual in particular, however, namely, Mr William Johnston, banker, has exerted himself much of late, and even sacrificed a considerable sum of money, to have the white-fishing on this coast turned to more account, and, it is to be hoped, with some prospect of final success.'

The fishing boats *Annabelle, Silver Chord* and *Girl Maureen* at the harbour. Fishing was still an important industry to the town by the 1950s with around forty boats of varying sizes operating and some two hundred men employed, mostly on a timeshare basis. Often the boat and gear would be owned by one man who acted as skipper employing four or five local men to act as crew and they would catch herring, cod, skate, mackerel, clams, ling and lobsters. Salmon were also netted at the mouth of the river, a practice recorded as far back as 1794 in the *Statistical Account of Scotland*: 'The Girvan is frequented by salmon, and for a long period there has been a considerable fishing at the mouth of it, held, under Crown charters, by the proprietor of the estate of Dunure on the north side. In former times, the mode of taking the salmon was by net and coble, but now stake-nets are substituted. Till very lately, the regular fishers experienced no interference on the part of the public; but for two or three years past, people have taken the liberty of putting down, what are called bag-nets all along the coast, and even on the ground formerly claimed by the proprietors, and in that way have killed a great many fish. This inroad is naturally enough opposed by the proprietors, and the matter is just now before the law courts, but as yet undecided.'

Holidaymakers queue patiently to hire one of the boats for a leisurely hour rowing around the calm waters of the harbour or up the river. The old whitewashed buildings, known locally as 'The Folly' or 'The Follies', that stood on the north side of Knockcushan Street opposite Knockcushan House, were demolished in the years between 1910 and 1912. As a direct result of this Knockcushan Gardens were created which offered panoramic views over the river, the harbour and Newton Kennedy. According to historians, Robert the Bruce reputedly held court at Knockcushan in 1328 and a memorial plaque commemorates this, while from the period 1186 to 1639 it was in continual use as the old Moot Hill, being the chief court of the Bailliary of Carrick. Knockcushan Street was known locally as 'the knowes' with the name being derived from the Gaelic knock, a hill, and 'cuish', a court of law. It was the sandy knowe where 700 years ago the Earls of Carrick held their feudal councils.

One of the main attractions for many visitors to Girvan was the opportunity to go on a cruise from the harbour across the Clyde and around Ailsa Craig. In the early 1900s the *Lady Ailsa* ferried passengers back and forth to 'The Craig', as it is known locally, and in 1924 it was replaced by another steamship, also called *Lady Ailsa*. However, the service proved to be unprofitable and in 1932 the vessel was sold and replaced two years later by this motorboat, the *Carrick Lass*. This vessel was renamed the *Lady Ailsa* and operated on the route until 1955 when it was replaced by a much smaller fishing-style boat. In the background are the workshops in Newton Kennedy that later became Alexander Noble and Sons' boatbuilding and repair yard.

Looking east along Ailsa Street West towards the McKechnie Institute on Dalrymple Street. The photographer was standing at the junction of Henrietta Street with the entrance to the Assembly Rooms visible on the right displaying posters advertising upcoming shows. On the left two soldiers in uniform can be seen walking past Queenslea Villas towards the Green, while further along the street on the right can be seen the junctions of Greenside and Wilson Street. The Assembly Rooms were built for and formerly occupied by the Rev. P. Hately Waddell's small congregation, which became known in Girvan as the 'Waddellites'. Aged 27, Waddell had arrived in the town during the time of the Disruption in 1843 and the following year established the independent Reforming Protestant Church with a congregation of around 200. Waddell led them for eighteen years and was also known as a writer, lecturer and biographer of Robert Burns. The Assembly Rooms were later demolished and the Catholic Hall now occupies the site.

In his book *Places of Interest About Girvan* (1892), the Rev. R. Lawson described the Doune Burn as being 'a spring of excellent water at the south end of the town, rising about 30 feet behind the wall through which it issues. In days when Girvan was not so well supplied with water as it is now, the Doune Burn was of prime importance, and was much frequented. Like all natural springs, the water is cooler and fresher than that brought in pipes, and it is still largely used, especially in hot weather. A friend has measured the flow of water for me, and found it to be a little over nine gallons per

minute, and this is never perceptibly diminished.' The spring was located at the south end of Dalrymple Street and in this photograph of it one of the local taverns is also visible. The *Ayrshire Directory* published in 1837 listed the Star Inn and livery stables on High Street with John Clachar, innkeeper; the Weaver's Arms on Doune Park with John Harvey, innkeeper; the King's Arms Inn and livery stables with Thomas Lyle, innkeeper; and the Buck's Head on Dalrymple Street with Elizabeth McKissock, innkeeper. No mention is made of the Ship Inn that once stood in Old Street and which was reputed to have been visited by Robert Burns. By the 1890s two further public houses were located on Dalrymple Street – the Crystal Palace and the Standard Vaults.

Looking east along Hamilton Street up the brae towards Church Square with the Provost's Lantern just discernable in front of the house in the centre. This was a large, ornamental paraffin street lantern that was erected in memory of one of the burgh's provosts. On the right is the shop owned by David Murray, the plumber, while next door is Funal's shop advertising all manner of refreshments such as tobacco, cigarettes, chocolate and ice cream. Across the street the gable advertises William Paterson, painter and decorator, H. Motion, the baker, and William Lennox, the plumbers. As recently as the early 1960s the town had as many as six bakers, five butchers, eleven cafes, four chemists, seven coal merchants, five confectionary shops, seven drapers, five fish-and-chip shops, three fishmongers, five general newsagents, eleven public houses, seven shoemakers, four watchmakers, five dairies, three children's shops, four gift shops, two wool shops, four electrical shops and eleven general grocers. There were in total something like 126 shops; today the number is less than half that.

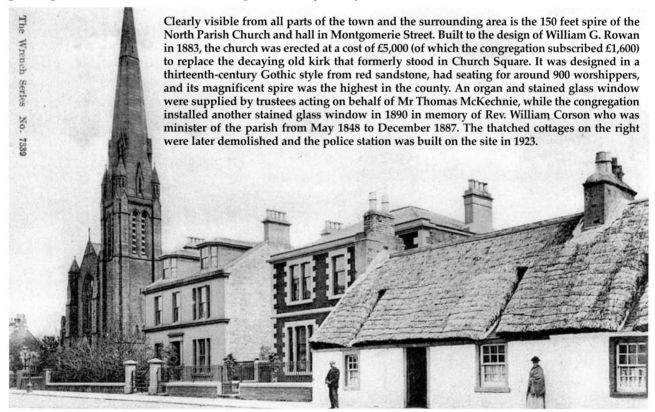

Clearly visible from all parts of the town and the surrounding area is the 150 feet spire of the North Parish Church and hall in Montgomerie Street. Built to the design of William G. Rowan in 1883, the church was erected at a cost of £5,000 (of which the congregation subscribed £1,600) to replace the decaying old kirk that formerly stood in Church Square. It was designed in a thirteenth-century Gothic style from red sandstone, had seating for around 900 worshippers, and its magnificent spire was the highest in the county. An organ and stained glass window were supplied by trustees acting on behalf of Mr Thomas McKechnie, while the congregation installed another stained glass window in 1890 in memory of Rev. William Corson who was minister of the parish from May 1848 to December 1887. The thatched cottages on the right were later demolished and the police station was built on the site in 1923.

The Festival of the Ayr Presbytery Choir Union at the North Parish Church, 11 June 1904. The graveyard on Old Street just north of the Flushes contains the remains of Girvan's first parish church, which was approximately 50 feet long by 28 feet wide and could accommodate roughly 500 people. In 1780 this was replaced by a new church which was built on a more prominent position overlooking the town at the top of Hamilton Street. It was reached via the Kirk Brae and in front of it stood the Market Cross. This building was demolished in 1883 and replaced by the present church seen here.

Looking north along Henrietta Street from the grass of Stair Park around 1910 with the Queen's Jubilee water fountain visible in the foreground. The gable end of the South Parish Church, built in 1842, is also on the left. In the distance along Henrietta Street it is just possible to make out the Public School building followed by the Assembly Rooms. In the 1850s the South Parish Church was known as the 'Kirk on the Green', there being no houses at that time on both Henrietta Street and Louisa Drive. The junction with Duncan Street is on the right, across the street from the church and the fountain; this street was named after Admiral Duncan who was responsible for a famous victory over the Dutch fleet at Camperdown in 1797 and became a national hero. He had strong connections with the local Bargany family and his daughter Jane married Sir Hew Dalrymple Hamilton on 14 May 1800. Admiral Sir Frederick Dalrymple Hamilton of Bargany, a descendant of Admiral Duncan, was in command of HMS *Rodney* during the sinking of the *Bismarck* in 1941.

Assembled on the grass of Stair Park opposite the houses on Henrietta Street is 'D' Company of the 18th Highland Light Infantry. The 18th was raised in Glasgow on 26 February 1915 by the Lord Provost as a bantam battalion and went to the Girvan Camp shortly afterwards where many local men were also enlisted. Bantam battalions were authorised for those men who were below the official height limits of enlistment. In June 1915 the men were moved to Gailes and in August to Salisbury Plain. The men were sent to France and Flanders in February 1916. Later, they became known as the 18th (Royal Glasgow Yeomanry) Battalion, the Highland Light Infantry. The 26 battalions of the Highland Light Infantry as a whole saw action in France, Belgium, the Dardanelles, Egypt, Palestine and Mesopotamia.

This photograph from the mid 1930s shows the view from Church Square looking down the brae into Hamilton Street towards 'Auld Stumpy' at the Cross and into Knockcushan Street, or 'the Knowes' as it was frequently known. 'Auld Stumpy' is the town steeple, built in 1825–27 for use as the town gaol, a purpose it fulfilled until the 1870s. It remains a key landmark and is open to the public at certain times during the summer. A bus of the Ayrshire Pullman Motor Services negotiates around the attractive McCubbin Fountain which was erected in 1911 and replaced the Provost's Lantern which stood for many years on this spot. The fountain was gifted to the town by Hugh McCubbin, a local benefactor, and it still occupies this position today. The bus stance was at Church Square and from here passengers could catch the bus to Maybole and then onwards to Ayr.

Looking south from the area known as the Flushes into Bridge Street and towards the Cross. On the right is the junction for the road that led to the bridge over the river into Newton Kennedy and also to the Manse. The premises owned by George A. Kydd, auctioneers, valuers and house furnishers, are also on the right; the premises were known locally as the Bridge House. Established in 1921, Kydd's were responsible for furnishing the council chambers within the McMaster Hall and in 1968 an advert within a local journal stated that the partners at that time were Sarah M. Kydd and manager Kenneth C. Kydd. Bridge Street, despite not having much of a bridge to boast of, originally took its name from the small bridge that once existed here spanning the Mill Burn. Today, the burn flows unnoticed under the main road.

Looking along Dalrymple Street from the Cross, with the entrance to the McMaster Hall (built in 1911) on the right. This is followed by the frontage of the King's Arms Hotel while the McKechnie Institute is further along. One of the main thoroughfares of the town, Dalrymple Street has always had numerous shops and cafes. In days gone by these included the Cabin at No. 54, which advertised itself as the 'best place in town for a good cup of tea'; for something to eat, William Davidson baker and confectioner at No. 131 was the place to go. He also had a shop at No. 15 Bridge Street and remarkably he had been awarded a hundred gold, silver and bronze medals and diplomas at various Glasgow and London exhibitions. Most notably he had received gold medals for his excellent pan bread, sponge goods, gingerbread, tea bread, meringues, puff and tart pastries, plain cakes and Scotch buns.

Dalrymple Street pictured in the early 1900s, looking north towards the McKechnie Institute on the left which was built in 1888. On the left is James Crosbie's ironmonger's shop while across the road is the distinctive cupola frontage of the Tower Warehouse. In the early 1800s John Duff was the appointed Town-Officer of Girvan and he was frequently seen walking through the principal streets ringing his bell and shouting out loudly for all to hear – 'Gather unto me, all ye ends of the earth!' He also entertained the inhabitants with rhymes such as 'Fresh cod and saut cod/mackerel and skate/to be sold at Matthew Sloan's/at a reasonable rate'! John was however also particular to a strong drink and a friend who kept a licensed house once cautioned him with the old proverb, 'Every glass you drink is a nail in your coffin.' Mocking this statement, every time John ordered his favourite tipple, he would simply ask for 'Tippence worth o' coffin nails'.

Looking north along Dalrymple Street, probably in the 1940s, with Crosbie's Ironmongers and the Maybole Shoe Shop (est. 1826) visible on the left, followed by the junction of Ailsa Street West. The distinctive octagonal frontage of the McKechnie Institute, which was opened in December 1888, is also on the left while across the road can be seen W.K. Blair's pharmacy and the Tower Warehouse selling knitwear and hosiery. Further along the street can be seen the trees that mark the site of Chalmers United Free Church which was built in 1857. Other shops within the town at this time were A.L. Colvin, draper at No. 48 Dalrymple Street and 'the keenest cash drapery store in Girvan'; D. & S. Nisbet, booksellers at No. 8 Knockcushan Street; and T.E. Browne and Sons, 'leaders in the field of up-to-date attractions for half a century', with 'pastimes' in Dalrymple Street and 'amusements' at the seafront.

Park End and Cauldshore are located in the south of the town. The photographer is standing on Bennane Road looking northwards into Kirkpatrick Street with the new houses on Henrietta Street visible in the distance. On the left is the junction of Cauldshore while on the right the road sweeps into Glendoune Street. The names of the old streets were all connected to fishing and smuggling, which was carried on as eagerly here as at Ballantrae and Kirkoswald. In the eighteenth century the same receptacles were to be found for concealing contraband goods – brandy holes in the fields and cellars under the kitchen floors. So plentiful was cognac that one morning a farmer's wife mistook it for well water when making the porridge; it was noticed that the men supped more porridge than usual that morning! Coalpits and Coalshore, now corrupted into Coalpots and Cauldshore, took their names from a seam of coal that was wrought there many years ago (although at a loss).

The houses on Henrietta Street were completed in October 1921 by the burgh council and marked the start of an extensive house building project aimed at easing the severe shortage of homes within Girvan during the inter-war years. Upon completion of the houses sycamore trees surrounded by metal railings were planted at regular intervals along the roadside to create an attractive avenue leading into the town.

A.F. Ross & Sons' motor garage and blacksmiths was located where Glendoune Street joined the Bennane Road, which in this photograph can be seen leaving the town with the houses of Shallochpark visible in the distance. On the left are the metal railings of the Doune School whilst just out of picture on the right is the junction of Cauldshore Street. Although the motor car gave people a greater sense of freedom to travel down to the shore at Girvan for the day it also allowed many to explore the surrounding countryside. Congestion caused by the steady increase in traffic along the coastal route saw numerous accidents in and around the town and the *Ayr Advertiser* of 12 August 1915 reported a 'Motor Accident – At the junction of Vicarton Street and Montgomerie Street, Girvan, on Thursday afternoon, a motor cycle proceeding out of the town collided with the rear mudguard of a motor car coming in the opposite direction. The cycle was somewhat damaged and the rider, Mr William McClinden, medical student, residing at Kilgrammie Schoolhouse, Dailly, sustained injuries to his face and left hand. He was conveyed home in a motor car.'

In 1860 the railway line from Glasgow and Ayr finally reached Girvan but originally only ran to a small terminus just north of Old Street. The line was later extended across the Water of Girvan into Newton Kennedy and down to the harbourside where special sidings were built for the unloading of coal at high tide into waiting vessels for export to Ireland. Following the completion in 1877 of the line from Girvan to Stranraer, known as the Girvan & Portpatrick Junction Railway, a new station, seen here, was built at the east end of Vicarton Street. After being hampered for many years by financial and operational difficulties, the line was taken over and renamed the Ayrshire & Wigtownshire Railway in 1887, but only five years later was taken over again by the Glasgow & South Western Railway, with the line being known as the Ayr & Stranraer Branch. The old station and line down to the harbourside became known as the Girvan Goods & Harbour Branch.

Young children paddling on the sands at Girvan in the early 1900s. The long sandy beach was a big attraction for visitors, as was the town's beautiful location, as described in an old journal of 1916 which was quoted in editions of the *Kilmarnock Standard* in January and February 1926: 'The town suffers little from cold east winds, for its site is only a short distance from a semicircle of four hills – Saugh Hill, Piedmont Hill, Dow Hill, and Byne Hill. The two hills at the extremities are considerably higher than the two in the centre. In front of the town is the restless tumbling sea. On a clear day the eye can range from the Cowal Hill on the north to the blue line of Antrim in the south. Slightly to the southward, Ailsa, locally known as the Craig, stands out boldly; northwards we see Pladda and the mainland of Arran as far north as Holy Isle, with the splendid peaks of the northern part of the island rising high into the air. Behind these the view is bounded by the long line of Cantyre. On the Ayrshire side every bend of the coast can be seen over a distance of fifteen miles between Turnberry and Bennane, while inland the valley of the Girvan affords a pleasing prospect.'

Races and fun days were often held down on the beach during the summer months and in this photograph from 15 May 1913 it appears that a sandcastle competition is well underway. The *Carrick Herald* of August 1926 reported on such a 'Sand Building Competition': 'Under the auspices of the *Daily Mail*, and in association with the Girvan Attractions Committee, a sand castle building competition took place on the South Beach, Girvan, yesterday. The little architects began at ten o'clock, and towards noon there was a fine display of work, there being no fewer than 125 competitors.' The designs were described as being both original and very cleverly executed and included the winning theme of 'King and Country' (although the article did not say how this was expressed in the design), an American skyscraper, and bells.

This photograph shows the large chute that was built opposite the bathing station and just out of picture on the left was the wooden lifeguard/diving platform. Born in 1831, the Rev. Roderick Lawson wrote many books recounting the history of Girvan and places within Ayrshire such as Maybole, Ailsa Craig and Crossraguel Abbey. His father was a rope-spinner within the town and Roderick received his early education at the old parish school in Henrietta Street. In 1864 he became minister of the West Parish Church in Maybole and lived there until his death in 1907. He travelled extensively throughout Scotland, going as far north as the Shetland Islands and also overseas to India. Among his works, is the poem entitled 'Bonnie Girvan Shore' and one memorable verse reads: 'I've seen the sun in other lands/Rise flashing from the sea/ I've seen it set, at close of day/ In crimson majesty/ But ne'er a sunset have I seen/ Search all the wide world o'er/ Like the sunsets seen on Arran's heights/ From bonnie Girvan shore.'

The boating pond, pictured in the early 1950s. On the left are the large villa-style houses on Louisa Drive which overlook the shore, while on the right, on a small island within the pond, are the gliderdrome and trampolines. The boating pond was always very popular after it opened in 1938 and is still used occasionally during the summer months.

The putting greens were adjacent to the boating pond. Overlooking the Green, the large villas on Louisa Drive were built in the 1890s. The Green was a large area of common grass where the lifeboat was once launched by horse and cart into the water and it was also where people used to dry their laundry and fishermen their nets. In the right background is the war memorial, erected in 1922 in the middle of Stair Park, and beyond that are the council houses on Henrietta Street, built around the same time. On the very far right is the ornamental bandstand and tea rooms that were built next to the wall of the Doune Cemetery and the old gas works. Prior to the war memorial, a large flagstaff occupied the central position within Stair Park for many years.

The model yacht pond was another tourist attraction located down by the harbourside on the Green, adjacent to the boating lake and gliderdrome (far right) which are visible in this photograph from the early 1940s. Notice the wooden cradles in the foreground which were used to carry the model yachts down to the water. On Thursday 15 August 1915, the *Ayr Advertiser* reported on the unfortunate 'Death of a Glasgow Visitor' – 'A young married man, a Glasgow visitor, residing at 34 Harbour Street, Girvan, died on Wednesday night under tragic circumstances. It appears that while coughing, he accidentally swallowed his false teeth. Medical aid was procured, and, acting upon the advice of the medical man, the visitor underwent an operation, but all efforts to save his life were unavailing.'

The tennis courts and bowling greens, pictured in May 1913, were part of the Morton Recreational Grounds, named after Mr William Morton of Ardmillan Castle who donated 1,000 guineas to the bowling club to provide sporting facilities. There were four bowling greens and six hard tennis courts as well as a croquet lawn. In the background is the North Parish Church on Montgomerie Street with its towering spire and 'Auld Stumpy' at the Cross. The large greenhouses belong to the nursery owned by Alan Balch, which specialised in cut flowers, tomatoes, strawberries and fresh vegetables with wreaths and bouquets also being made to order.

Girvan Bowling Club was formed on 21 July 1841 and moved to new greens located just off The Avenue in 1897. There were originally two greens here but in 1938 green No. 3, named Trochrague, was laid down and eleven years later green No. 4, named Dalquharran, was also created. The clubhouse was extended and modernised in 1961 to incorporate a small veranda, lounge and changing rooms. In August 2001 the World Blind Bowling Championships were held within Scotland for the very first time at Girvan and players from ten different countries around the globe attended. Located at No. 37 The Avenue, it is estimated that over 2,000 visitors from all over the world are attracted annually to the town to play on the greens. This photograph shows the clubhouse and flagstaff, and No.1 green, Bargany. The spire of the North Parish Church is in the left background, while on the right are the houses of Montgomerie Street.

Looking north from an upstairs window at the back of one of the houses on Bridge Street, with the Water of Girvan meandering its way down towards the harbour. In the foreground is the road bridge crossing the river into Newton Kennedy where fishing nets can be seen drying on the grass with the wooden fishing boats drawn up along the water's edge. Further upstream a train with trucks laden with coal is crossing the railway bridge to reach the sidings that were constructed down by the harbourside. The goods station is also visible on the right while the houses on Watermouth Park, now known as Golf Course Road, can be seen sweeping round to the gentle hill that is known locally as Knockavally. This scene has since changed greatly, with Noble's Boat Building and Repair Yard now occupying most of the foreground area. Following the closure of the Girvan Goods and Harbour Branch of the Glasgow & South Western Railway, the railway bridge was dismantled and the goods station demolished, with that area of land now becoming the site of Strathavon Caravan Park.

According to the old journal of 1916, serialised in the *Kilmarnock Standard* in 1926, there 'are some interesting historical facts relating to the bridge over the Girvan at the north end of the town'. It was known as the 'Brig of Girwand' and 'we note that a bridge had existed there at the end of the sixteenth century, which must have gone to ruin, or been swept away, less than a hundred years after; for at the beginning of the year 1696 we find the Presbytery of Ayr supplicating Lord Bargany, the patron, to build another bridge, as lives had been lost by churchgoers trying to cross the river after a spate. His lordship was in no hurry. After some years, however, the present bridge was built after a special Act had been passed by the Scottish Parliament to enable Bargany to defray the expense out of teinds belonging to vacant charges in Maybole and Colmonell.' The 'Brig of Girwand' stood a short way above the position of the old railway bridge (since dismantled) which was formerly used to bring carriages down to the specially built sidings at the harbour side. This photograph shows the Newton Kennedy road bridge that carries traffic over the river into Newton Kennedy which is visible on the right. Newton Kennedy, which was once known as 'Ower the Water', was named after the Laird of Dalquharran who owned the land on that side of the river for many years.

A view from May 1913, looking northeast out over the New Half Golf Course from the large villas that were built around 1900 on Watermouth Park. In the foreground is the narrow road that ran along the bottom of the gardens and through the course to join the main road. The Water of Girvan can be seen winding its way slowly down through the course to the harbour, while in the distance is the Bridge Mill among the trees and on the right are the signalman's tower and large water tank which marked the site of the Girvan Junction. This was where trains on the line were diverted onto the Girvan Goods & Harbour Branch of the line which ran behind Old Street to the Goods Station and onto the sidings at the harbourside in Newton Kennedy. The golf course is some 80 acres in extent and is described as not too demanding but with a beautiful backdrop of sea on one side and hills on the other. The first eight holes and oldest part of the course are alongside the shore whilst the remaining newer holes, seen here, are inland beside the river, hence the name 'New Half'. Just out of view on the left was the rising ground once known as 'Knock-o'-Vallie' (or the 'the hill of the Bailie') which stands close to the Gallowhill. Today it is called Golf Course Hill.

Bridge Mill was located on the banks of the Water of Girvan at the junction of the main coastal road and the road to Dailly. The large weir was further upstream with a lade running down to the mill. The water wheel, which is visible in this photograph, was a large breast paddle five feet wide and creating from 25–30 horsepower depending on the weather and the strength of the current in the river. The mill building was four storeys in height which enabled large hoppers to be used and there were four pairs of stones used for grinding oatmeal and corn. The kiln was potted and held about a ton of oats whilst a sack tackle was used to haul heavy sacks to the upper floors. In 1947 the mill was owned by Hutchinson and McCreath Ltd, grain merchants. Today, the site is occupied by Ross's motor garage.

Trochrague, or Trochrig, dates from 1803 when it was the family seat of the Boyd family. It is located to the northeast of Girvan and in the years 1910–23 the mansion was substantially altered by J.J. Burnett with the addition of a porte cochere above the front entrance and also a tall tower. Both are visible in this photograph dating from the late 1950s when Trochrague was being run as a private guesthouse by the Sisters of St Joseph of Cluny. The house was donated to them in 1957 by the then owners, the Todd family, and in 1993 the mansion house was again gifted to the recently founded Jericho Benedictine religious order who continue to run it as a guesthouse.

The walled gardens of Trochrague House are located to the east at Nether Trochrague where the art of topiary was frequently practiced by the gardeners. In 1852 a stone mould which had been used for casting bronze articles was found near the mansion house. It is oval in shape and on one side there are moulds for five different articles – a ring, a seal and three other articles the use of which cannot be determined. On the other side there is a large compartment with a chequered surface and this is open at one end. The mould is made of green serpentine, a stone found down the coast at Bennane in abundance and which is well suited for making into moulds. This was one of only two Bronze Age stone moulds to have been discovered within Ayrshire.

Blair House is located four miles northeast of Girvan off the road to Dailly and is a Victorian mansion house built from red sandstone. The house is reached along a long driveway and commands an elevated south-facing position overlooking the Girvan valley and is situated within a small estate. This view is of the front of the house with the terraced lawns which lead down to a pond and the summer house. On the right is the extension containing the billiard room and the large conservatory, while behind the house is Blair farmhouse and an adjoining cottage. This photograph was taken around 1905 and used on a postcard; it was sent to a Miss Harrison in Ilford, Essex, and the message reads, 'Thank you so much for your nice long letter, will write soon, this is the house I am staying in. Lots of Love. Yours E.B.'

Assembled in the PE hall is one of the girls' classes of the Secondary Department of Girvan High School, which was opened in 1912 and located in Henrietta Street. Girvan had four official schools during Victorian times: the parish school, with its stone belfry, built in 1832 and renovated in 1911; the Burgh School, built in 1875 in Henrietta Street; the infant school on the Green where the old High School now stands; and the Doune School at the south end of the town. The High School provided secondary education until a new building was opened in Wesley Road in 1955. In 1989 Girvan Academy opened on The Avenue and the Wesley Road building became occupied by the primary and nursery schools. In the logbook of the parish school, session 1863/64, it was noted that 'September 23: An unusual number of scholars absent today – probable cause; the eating of fruits. October 7: A good deal of punishing today for want of lessons. October 27: A good deal of strapping today for carelessness in writing. May 30: The master, having ascertained that an absentee had been sent to school in the morning, despatched two officers of justice to apprehend the truant. The latter, however, having espied them in the distance, got safely ensconced under the blankets and his too compassionate mamma refused to give him up.'

Glendoune is an attractive late Georgian mansion house that can be found surrounded by woodland just to the southwest of Girvan at the foot of the Doune Glen. Built in 1800, on the site of an old religious chapel, for Spencer Boyd of Penkill, it was sold in 1845 to the Right Hon. T.F. Kennedy of Dunure who sold it almost straight away to George Kirkpatrick Young. Young added the high Italianate wing that is visible to the right of the entrance front but never built the planned wing on the left side of the house. The mansion house remained in the Young family until 2007 when it was placed on the market with a price of £1,000,000. This included the house, its policies, the attractive walled garden to the rear and an adjoining cottage. Glendoune means 'the glen of the forts' and the mansion house sits directly below the Doune Hill facing west out towards the sea. The estate was formerly named Piedmont and this survives in the name of Piedmont Road which now leads directly from the town to the estate.

Nestling at the foot of the Byne Hill about two and a half miles south of Girvan is the mansion house of Ardmillan. Originally a sixteenth-century tower house, Ardmillan was the property of the Kennedys of Bargany from 1476 but later passed through marriage to the Crawfords of Baidland in 1658. The castle was visited by Mary, Queen of Scots, in 1563. Ardmillan Castle was extended throughout the eighteenth century to form an attractive mansion house with a Georgian wing. It was described by the Rev. R. Lawson as being 'quaint and picturesque, nestling cosily among its woods at the foot of the hill, and looking out over the ever-varying panorama of the Firth of Clyde.' Ardmillan was also said to contain one of the most elegant drawing rooms in the county. In 1855, James Crawford of Ardmillan became Lord Ardmillan, the well known Scottish judge and Lord of Session. The castle and estate eventually passed to the Playfairs in the late nineteenth century, who sold it in turn to Mr Morton, a native of the Irvine Valley, who had made a large fortune in England in the boot trade. The castle suffered from a fire in 1910 and again in 1972, which resulted in the death of the then lady owner. In 1991 the remains of the castle and mansion house were demolished and replaced by a caravan site.

This photograph from around 1915 possibly shows Mr Morton, who owned one of the first motor cars in the district, at the mansion house of Ardmillan. In nearby Girvan, Mr Robert Dickie opened the town's first garage in Old Street and he was the sole agent for Rover. Many of the first motor vehicles in the district bore registration plates with only a single letter code of G followed by numbers which denoted that the car was registered in Glasgow. From 1921 onwards, when these numbers became exhausted, the SD suffix was adopted for Ayrshire.

Rising to a height of 214 metres, Byne Hill dominates the view to the south of Girvan and this photograph has captured the hill after a heavy snowfall in December 1908. A similar view was described by the Rev. R. Lawson in his book *Views of Carrick*, published in 1894: 'The Byne Hill is the most conspicuous landmark about Girvan. This view of it is taken from a point rather more than two miles from the town, and forms, in my judgement, one of the prettiest peeps in the neighbourhood. The Byne Burn flows at its foot. The Lover's Loaning skirts it. The Bride's Bed hangs on its flank. Woodland Bay acts as its mirror, while Craig Skelly and the Skart Rock serve as break-waters, and high and steep over all towers the Byne itself, the genius of the place, which fills all eyes with its presence.'

Pictured in the early 1900s, three horsedrawn stagecoaches of the Girvan and Ballantrae Coaching Tour, travelling south on the main road, stop at Kennedy's Pass en route to Lendalfoot to admire the magnificent views. Passengers were picked up at the King's Arms Hotel in Girvan which was the headquarters of the coaching tours, run by Thomas Lees. The main coastal road that ran from Girvan to Ballantrae followed the shoreline and in places where the cliffs were too steep and rocky it headed inland and along the hillside. One such place was just south of Girvan near Kilranny where the road climbed inland and along the hillside before descending down to the coast again at Slockenray. Kennedy's Pass took its name from the Right Hon. T.F. Kennedy of Dalquharran who, in 1831, authorised the building of a new road lower down along the coast which meant that some of the rocky cliffs had to be blasted away to make a path for the route. Despite the main road having been widened considerably over the years, the large, protruding boulder of rock, visible on the left of this image, can still be seen today.

**The Water of Lendal enters the sea at the small coastal hamlet of Lendalfoot some seven miles south of Girvan. The Bay of Lendal was once a favourite haunt of smugglers and later supported a number of small inshore fishermen. The striking ruins of Carleton Castle, perched on a rocky ridge, overlook Lendalfoot and the Bay of Lendal. It dates from the fifteenth century and was formerly five storeys in height and there was also once a surrounding courtyard with small towers. It was a stronghold of the Cathcarts of Carleton, who were a powerful and influential family in this part of Ayrshire. Adjacent is Little Carleton Farm with Balsalloch Hill in the background.**

*Right*: On the bank of the Lendal Water at Lendalfoot stands the monument erected to the memory of Charles Berry. Born in 1872, Charles was a self-taught naturalist and ornithologist who lived in one of the small cottages earning a living from lobster fishing. Often he would be seen walking in the evenings with a gun under his arm, or a moth net in his hand, busily hunting for specimens to add to his collection. He collected nearly 200 different species of bird eggs, all the common local species of British moths, many stuffed specimens of rare birds, all the various kinds of crustaceans to be found along the shore and what was often described as being a 'heterogenous collection of curiosities', including precious stones, minerals and fossils. He contributed frequently to the Paisley Museum and was also the first person to predict accurately the arrival of the migrant Wheatear bird to Scotland each summer. Charles died on 1 February 1909, aged just 36 years, and was buried in Colmonell graveyard where his tombstone is decorated with carvings of a bird in a nest and a plant growing over a rock.

*Left*: The Boar's Head hotel on Colmonell's Main Street, photographed around 1905. This was the first hotel to greet the traveller on the main road from Ballantrae as they entered the village on a sharp turn in the road to the left known locally as the 'Kirk Wynd'. It was a popular stopping off place for the horse-drawn coaches of the Ballantrae Coaching Tour, with many of their passengers choosing to stay and enjoy the beautiful scenery in the glen of the River Stinchar. Another hotel in Colmonell at that time was the Queen's Hotel, located further along Main Street. The Boar's Head Hotel is still in business today.

Dalreoch House was built to the east of Colmonell, at the base of Dalreoch Hill on the opposite bank of the River Stinchar from the village. James Paterson in his *History of the County of Ayr*, published in 1847, related that, 'there was formerly an old house or castle at Dalreoch which existed in 1696, the property and seat of the MacAlexanders, who possessed, at one time, considerable property in Carrick.' He also writes that, 'at Dalreoch, there was once a cave on the hillside, in which the proprietors often found shelter from the soldiery. This circumstance gave rise to a belief amongst the peasantry that the hill was the abode of fairies. The cave has now been expanded into a quarry' (and today little trace now exists). This refers to John MacAlexander who, along with a great many others, was detained and then subsequently discharged for not attending the Raid at Dumfries in 1600. He was on Bargany's side in the bitter feudal fight with the Earl of Cassillis at Pennyglen in 1601. His name also occurs in the list of persons denounced by the Privy Council for appearing in arms on that occasion and he was again denounced for the same cause in 1607.

The Ford House stands on the banks of the River Stinchar at Colmonell and marks the site of the ancient ford where travellers once crossed the River Stinchar to reach Bardrochat, Craigneil and Herensford. This is the view looking upstream as the river sweeps gently round and flows under the Stinchar Bridge, which is just out of picture to the left. In April 1867 the County Road Trustees granted £1,560 to the Girvan District Trustees to enable them to rebuild and extend the bridge that existed here on the road that ran southwards from Colmonell. The twin-arched bridge was designed by Hugh and Bryce McCall, surveyors of Girvan, and the main contract was awarded to Andrew Murray who was a stone mason, also in Girvan. A temporary bridge was constructed from wood for the convenience of travellers while the old one was broken apart and the new one constructed. Freestones were brought all the way from Thornhill in Dumfriesshire, granite from Dalbeattie, and wood from both Stranraer and Ballantrae. A derrick crane was also constructed on site to enable the masons to lever the large stones into position. Today the bridge still carries traffic over the river. In this photograph from the early 1900s, Bardrochat House is visible high up on the hill overlooking the river and Colmonell.

Near the entrance to the village stand the ivy-clad ruins of Kirkhill Castle and the fine Elizabethan-styled mansion house of Kirkhill. Dating from around 1843–45, Kirkhill House was built by David Rhind for Lieutenant Colonel Barton of Ballaird, a hero of the Battle of Waterloo in 1815. Separated by only a matter of feet are the ruins of the tower house erected in 1589 by Thomas Kennedy and his wife Janet when the Kennedys of Bargany acquired the land after the Reformation. The castle bears the inscription 'T.K. 1589, J.K.' and cut into a stone placed above the door are also the arms of the husband and wife (although so worn by the weather that it is almost impossible to make them out). The castle is in ruins but in a good state of preservation. There are also large mounds of earth in the glebe at the front of the castle; these were obviously intended to defend the ford across the River Stinchar. A descendant of the family was Sir Thomas Kennedy of Kirkhill who became Lord Provost of Edinburgh in 1680.

Bardrochat House occupies an elevated position overlooking the village and the Stinchar Valley. It was built in 1893 from red sandstone, with unusual bell-capped round towers and an attractively curved Dutch-styled gable, by the architect George Mackie Watson for Robert Finnie McEwen, a noted philanthropist. The house was extended in 1906–08 by Robert Lorimer and inside there was a large drawing room, conservatory, dining room, sitting room and a large wooden-panelled entrance hall and stairs. Within the surrounding policies there was also a croquet lawn, walled gardens and a tennis court, while attached to Bardrochat Estate was a small gamekeeper's cottage called Oaknowe. On the Colmonell War Memorial is an inscription to James Robert Dundas McEwen, lieutenant in the 2nd Battalion of the Royal Scots Fusiliers who was killed in action 12 October 1916. Aged only 20, he was the son of Robert Finnie McEwen and Mary Frances McEwen of Bardrochat. Sir John McEwen also later became a notable politician and was MP for Berwick and Haddington from 1931–45 and in 1953 was created Baronet of Marchmont, the family's other seat in the Borders, and of Bardrochat. This photograph is of the side and rear of the house.

This is the view looking west out over the Stinchar Valley from the walled gardens at Bardrochat House. The ruins of Craigneil Castle are on the rocky knoll, while in the distance surrounded by trees is Knockdolian House on the banks of the River Stinchar. The view from Bardrochat House and the village was described as being one of the most picturesque and romantic within Ayrshire. '[Colmonell] stands on a rising ground above the Stinchar, looking down to the green hill of Knockdolian, and up to the woods of Pinmore, while in the horizon may be seen the lofty hills of Barr, and even of far away Galloway,' was the description given by the Rev. R. Lawson in 1892. This postcard was published by John Reeves who owned a small provisions store on Main Street adjacent to the Queen's Hotel. He frequently displayed boards outside his shop selling a number of postcards depicting local views.

Knockdolian Hill rises steeply to a height of 265 metres and is the largest hill in the district. The name means the 'hill of the storms' and according to local tradition it has often been called the 'Fause [false] Craig' due to its uncanny resemblance to Ailsa Craig in the Firth of Clyde. Being similar in appearance when viewed from the sea, especially when thick fog descends, tradition asserts that it has often lured mariners to their deaths on the rocky Ayrshire coastline. On the summit of the hill is a Bronze Age burial cairn while on its northern slope is an ancient dun or fort known as Dunniwick, once believed by locals to be 'round which the fairies used to dance on moonlight nights.' This view from around 1900 shows Knockdolian House nestling in the woods below the hill.

Knockdolian House was designed and built on a pleasant site overlooking the River Stinchar by the architect David Rhind for Alexander MacCubbin Cathcart of Genoch and Knockdolian in 1842. The estate of Knockdolian was acquired in the fifteenth century by Gilbert Graham, and from the Grahams it passed to the Kennedys of Kirkmichael who did not retain it long. Their successors were a family by the name of MacCubbin and through a daughter it passed to the Cathcarts in whose family it remained until the nineteenth century. At Knockdolian there were large stepping stones across the River Stinchar as well as a metal footbridge which is visible in this photograph. Describing the estate in the seventeenth century, Abercrombie wrote, '[it] is shown what art and industrie can do, to render a place, to which nature hath not been favourable, very pleasant, by planting of gardens, orchards, walks, and rows of trees, that surprise the beholder with things so far beyond expectation, in a countrey so wild and mountainous'.

In the grounds of Knockdolian, adjacent to the house, are the well preserved ruins of Knockdolian Castle which was built around the sixteenth century by the Graham family on the foundations of a much more ancient structure. It was later acquired by the MacCubbins of Cathcart who undertook extensive repairs to the castle and surrounding policies around the middle of the seventeenth century. It was the home of Fergus MacCubbin and his wife Margaret Kennedy at that time.

Ballantrae with Ailsa Craig in the distance, as viewed from above Garleffin in June 1928. In this scene the main road can be seen snaking its way north towards the bridge over the River Stinchar before turning sharply to the left and entering the village. Visible on the right, with its solitary remaining tower, are the ruins of Ardstinchar Castle perched on a small rocky knoll overlooking the road to Knockdolian and Colmonell, while the war memorial is clearly visible next to the bridge. Further along the main road is the Free Church with its steeple followed by the small ornamental steeple of the parish church, and on the far left are the trees surrounding the tombstones within the old churchyard just off Main Street at the Vennel. Little has changed with this scene today, with only the Free Church having been demolished and the site now occupied by a private house, and the main road no longer crosses the old twin-arched bridge over the Stinchar. It was deemed to be in an unsafe condition and a new bridge was built in 1964 just to the west of the old one.

A motorist travelling south on the main coastal road from Girvan passes through Park End just before reaching Ballantrae. Park End was just a few small houses on the shore side of the road and the photographer of this 1940s view was standing at the junction of a narrow track that led down along the shore to the small tidal harbour at Ballantrae. The houses of Park End were built on a natural raised beach that ran as far north as Bennane Head and it was on this ground that an eighteen-hole golf course once existed but this has been closed for many years. Just out of view on the left, atop the appropriately named Mill Hill, are the remains of a late seventeenth-century windmill which can be reached by following a path from the village.

This is the view looking south from the small harbour at Foreshore. On the left is the row of single-storey cottages built in the early nineteenth century by the Girvan Building Society for the fishermen and their families. Further along can be seen the mast of the semaphore signal station with the steeple of the parish church also visible whilst in the distance, above the steeple of the parish church, is Glenapp Castle surrounded by woodland. The photographer is standing on the stone wall of the L-shaped harbour pier looking out over the fisherman's nets drying on the shingle beach and the wooden fishing boats that have been drawn up onto the shore. The fishing trade proved to be very lucrative as described in the *Ordnance Gazetteer of Scotland* published between 1882 and 1885: 'Ballantrae is the centre of the south-western fishery district, in which, during 1879, there were cured 25,428 barrels of white herrings, besides 6882 cod, ling, and hake, taken by 569 boats of 1363 tons, the person employed being 952 fishermen and boys, 78 fish curers, 49 coopers, and some 800 others, while the total value of boats, nets and lines was estimated at £11, 375.'

A former coaching inn dating from around 1770, the King's Arms Hotel in Ballantrae's Main Street was a stopping place for weary travellers on the main coastal route from Ayrshire into Galloway. It was built with stone that was taken from the crumbling ruins of nearby Ardstinchar Castle. Refreshments and a night's accommodation could be had while horses would be rested in the stables. In this photograph a horse-drawn stagecoach is parked outside the hotel while visible on the side of the carriage is the name of the proprietor, Thomas Lees. He operated the famed 'Coast and Country' tours which ran daily from April to September and departed from the King's Arms Hotel in Dalrymple Street, Girvan. The tours took passengers down the coast through Lendalfoot to Ballantrae and then inland to Colmonell before returning to Girvan via Pinmore.

Looking east along Main Street in the summer of 1928 with the Royal Hotel visible on the left followed by the trees and steeple of the Free Church and Free Church manse. In the distance, just above the trees, is the top of the war memorial erected near the ruins of Ardstinchar Castle and overlooking the road bridge across the River Stinchar. On the opposite side of the street the bus to Girvan has stopped to pick up passengers outside the Ardstinchar Inn. In the late nineteenth century Ballantrae became a small seaside resort and was popular with visitors who wanted to enjoy the fresh sea air and avoid the hustle and bustle of town life.

A later view of Main Street, taken after the demolition of the Free Church. On the left is the Royal Hotel while across the street is the Ardstinchar Inn, followed by James McKissock's shop. Ballantrae was described in the *Ordnance Gazetteer of Scotland*, published between 1882 and 1885, as being 'thirteen miles SSW of its post-town Girvan, and 10 WSW of Pinwherry Station on the Girvan and Portpatrick Junction Railway; with one main street, it has a branch of the Commercial Bank, a hotel, a public hall and reading room, a post office with money order, savings bank and telegraph departments, a neat parish church (rebuilt 1819; 600 sittings), a Free Church, and a school, which, with accommodation for 219 children, had (1879) an average attendance of 143, and a grant of £100,115.'

The Hughes-Onslow Memorial tennis courts at Ballantrae are located just off Arrol Avenue and were named after their generous benefactors, the Hughes-Onslow family, who resided at nearby Laggan House and at Balkissock. Located on a wall within the parish church is an attractive monument to the memory of Major Denzil Hughes-Onlsow who was killed in action on 10 July 1916, aged 52 years, while serving with the 6th Battalion Dorsetshire Regiment. He was the son of Henry and Judith Hughes-Onslow who resided at Balkissock and the husband of Marion who lived at Laggan House. This monument was paid for by the family and also carries the names of all the men from the village who fell during the First World War. This is the view looking northwest over the houses that line Main Street, with Ailsa Craig visible on the horizon. The tennis courts are still open to the public today.

This view from the 1920s shows the ruins of Ardstinchar Castle, overlooking the twin arched bridge which carries the main road across the River Stinchar at Ballantrae. The bridge was completed in 1778 after five years of work. The masons who were engaged in the construction of the piers or 'land stools' of the bridge encountered several problems, which were described in the records of the road commissioners, published in the *Carrick Herald* in 1912: '. . . the north side land stool was founded on a rock, but they on trying the middle and south land stools could find no rock, and were obliged to dig down ten foot of loose gravel in the channel of the water till they found a clay, where they laid wooden frames to found on. This was done at great expense and after employing thirty men a day for several weeks for pumping the water it was found necessary to employ Mr Heatly the engineer for erecting a machine to draw the water, which drew four tons in six minutes . . .' When the piers were finally completed near the end of July 1776, the problems continued. The water began immediately to undermine them, and whinstones were used to fence and fortify them. The final cost of the bridge exceeded £756, making it by far the most expensive built by the Ayrshire commissioners in the eighteenth century. Part of the finance had been contributed by Sir John Cathcart of Carleton, John Hamilton of Bargany and Archibald Crauford of Ardmillan, all substantial and influential landowners in Carrick. It is commonly believed that stones from nearby Ardstinchar Castle were used in its construction but the minutes of the commissioners' record that the stones were brought by boat from a quarry at Culzean and were hewn on site. The bridge proved costly to maintain as the river repeatedly threatened to undermine the piers and to open a new channel to the south.

Balnowlart House is located two miles east from Ballantrae just off the main road to Colmonell. The name means the 'cottage or house between two rivers' and is an apt description of its location for close by the Water of Tig flows into the River Stinchar. Surrounded and completely hidden from view by a small woodland, it was built in 1905 by the architects J. Jerdan and Son in the traditional Scottish style but the house was later abandoned and is now in a deteriorating condition. Nearby on the low summit of Balnowlart Hill are the remains of a Bronze Age burial cairn.

On the banks of the Water of Tig near Heronsford, some three miles east from Ballantrae, stood the magnificent Laggan House. The Lands of Laggan, as the estate was known, were owned by Quintin and James Johnston and then later by Robert Rankin, a writer from Irvine, who in turn, sold them to trustees for the Earl of Stair. In 1845 the lands were sold to Charles MacGibbon, whose son was David MacGibbon (1831–1902), the noted architect and historian, and he designed and built the house in 1868 with additions and alterations being carried out eighteen years later. The MacGibbon family left Laggan House in 1902 and the property was purchased by Major Hughes-Onslow with an extension being built to the house by James Miller in 1914. The house had previously been known as Gurphur (or Garphar) but this name was abandoned in favour of Laggan House. It was lived in for many years by the Hughes-Onslow family and a memorial was erected within the estate to honour the memory of Major Denzil Hughes-Onslow, who was killed in action during the First World War. Most of the house was later demolished to leave only one wing and it is now virtually unrecognisable from this photograph. The land surrounding the house has also been converted into a country holiday park with caravans.

Located roughly three miles to the east of Ballantrae, the Hamlet of Herensford comprises a number of small cottages within the Tig Glen on the banks of the Water of Tig, a tributary of the River Stinchar. The cottages overlook a small stone bridge which crosses the water and the name is derived from the ford that once existed at this location. The cottages housed workers who were employed within the nearby Laggan House and Estate, known as the Lands of Laggan, and visible in the background of this view are the steep slopes of Knockdolian Hill.

Finnarts was the mansion or summerhouse of Robert F. Kennedy and was located on the west slopes of Glen App, overlooking the Water of App and Finnarts Bay. The house took its name from the nearby Finnarts Hill. The house has long since been demolished, with the doocot and the nearby farm the only remaining evidence of the estate.

Looking northwest over Barrhill from the small rocky outcrop known locally as 'the Craigs' in July 1929. On the right are the houses of Main Street and the spire of the Free Church. Further up the road, just outside the village, is the Memorial Hall (erected in 1924) while next to it is the public school. Protruding above the trees, just above the hall and school, is the distinctive tower of Arnsheen Church. In the distance, right of centre, is the large mansion house of Kildonan with its tall narrow chimneys, while on the left the road can be seen steadily climbing out of the village on its way past the house known as Gowlands, towards the small railway station at Cairnlea which is out of shot.

Barrhill was a fairly isolated and remote place prior to the nearby railway station opening in 1877, but after this many cottages were built on the Main Street as the village expanded. The building of large mansion houses at Kildonan, Corwar, Drumlamford and Clauchrie and the development and improvement of the surrounding estates all directly contributed to the establishment of the village. Many local people lived in the village and found employment on the surrounding estates and it is often said by locals that the only reason the railway was ever constructed to Barrhill was to carry the huge amount of raw materials needed for these estates and their lavish mansion houses!

Looking west along Main Street in November 1933. In the 1950s the *Third Statistical Account* recorded that Barrhill had no less than seven shops to cater for villagers and the surrounding rural population. There were two general merchants selling groceries, boots, and feeding stuffs for cattle, a general grocer and a baker, a butcher, a draper and stationer, two small confectionery shops and a small café with a tearoom which was run by a so-called 'incomer' from London. Vans also travelled regularly round the surrounding countryside selling their wares to the more remote farms and within the large estates, with one grocer even travelling a distance of 20 miles to Bargrennan and Glen Trool and then a further ten miles up the Rowantree Road to Barr. Barrhill also had a branch of the Union Bank, a post office with money order and savings bank departments, a medical surgery and two hotels, the Galloway Hotel and the Commercial Inn, both with seven-day licences. The Commercial Inn has since been renamed the Trout Inn and is still open today.

Looking east along Main Street in November 1933, towards the narrow bridge over the Cross Water and the Free Church beyond. Just out of view on the right is the minor road that leads up to Cairnlea Station which was opened by the Girvan and Portpatrick Junction Railway on 5 October 1877. The small two-platform station featured in *The Five Red Herrings*, a 1931 sleuth novel by Dorothy L. Sayers featuring her character Lord Peter Wimsey. The novel was adapted for television in 1975. The station was closed briefly in February 1882 and again for three months in 1886 and on Monday, 28 December 1908 was the scene of a tragic accident. In the height of a severe blizzard a train, called the 'wee bogie', left Barrhill at 4.15 p.m. only to become stuck in a large snow drift two miles south of the village. In what were dreadful conditions, the fireman made his way back to Barrhill to raise the alarm but the wooden carriages were buried under the heavy snowdrifts and the occupants trapped without any means of heating. It was not until the Wednesday that the carriages were dug out and the passengers freed, but sadly as a result of the cold one woman perished. The station remains open today.

The main road to Newton Stewart turns sharply to the left as it leaves Barrhill and then, after travelling a short distance, crosses the road bridge over the Duisk River and turns sharply to the right. The old tollhouse that stands at the first sweeping bend had been converted into a small garage with twin petrol pumps by the time of this photograph from July 1929. On the right is the junction of the Knowe Road that led to the old waulk mill with its tall chimney and Drumlamford House and then eventually over the exposed moors to Newton Stewart. In the distance can be seen the trees and shrubs that mark the course of the Duisk River and the main road which is out of view on the opposite bank. The gently sloping hill in the background was known as Blair Fell and had an ancient cairn on its slopes, while further along the main road was Blair Farm and the track that led to Black Clauchrie House.

Looking northwest along the main road as it leaves Barrhill, heading towards Pinwherry. The Memorial Hall is on the left with the war memorial just visible above the rooftop. Further along the main road is the public school. The junction of the road to Balluski and the Waulk Mill Bridge over the Duisk River is on the right. This single-track road also leads to the farm of Knockmalloch on the hilly slopes overlooking Kildonan Estate. It was here in 1789 that the poet and divine, John Burt, was born. He was learning the trade of a handloom weaver when he was pressed into joining the navy at the age of eighteen and served on board the *Magnificent* until 1812. By 1816 he was teaching at a school in Kilmarnock, but because of his part in a political agitation, he was forced to emigrate overseas to the United States to escape prosecution. He taught at Princetown College, became Presbyterian minister at Salem, and in 1835 was appointed to a theological professorship. He died on 24 March 1866, aged 77.

Glen Alty House was built in the early 1900s and is located just off a narrow country road known locally as the Knowe Road, about half a mile outside Barrhill. It is surrounded by wooded grounds and located at the rear is a coach house, a stable block for stabling three horses, and a small outbuilding for the storage of hay. The house was named after the Alty Burn, which flows down off the moorland surrounding Loch Alty in the surrounding hills and tumbles through the gardens and directly past the house. In this photograph dating from around the 1920s, the small footbridge that crossed the stream is visible on the right as well as the wall that guided the burn down past the house on its course to join the Duisk River.

Four miles southeast of Barrhill, Corwar House was built in 1838 for Mr Peter Rigby Wason and his wife Euphemia McTier by the architect W. Frazer, who eight years earlier had built nearby Drumlamford House. Rigby Wason, a native of Liverpool and at one time MP for Ipswich, had purchased the lands of Corwar, which for many generations had been the property and shooting ground of the Kennedys of Kirkmichael. The house was built from Creetown granite and a small lake, which its owners referred to as 'the pond', was also created close by. Wason was not only a successful barrister but also an innovative farmer as was noted in the *Ordnance Gazetteer of Scotland*, published in the early 1880s: 'The vales contain a good deal of fertile alluvial land,

and great improvements have been effected within the last 40 years, especially on the Corwar Estate, where fully 3,500 acres of wild heathery moor and 200 of deep moss have been reclaimed and now yield excellent pasturage.' The couple's son, John Cathcart Wason, also farmed and became a politician, serving as an MP in both Scotland and New Zealand. He was best remembered for having passed his time in the House of Commons knitting! In 1869 he purchased 20,000 acres on New Zealand's South Island and renamed it Corwar after his father's estate in Scotland and he also built a small village called Barrhill.

Formerly known as Drumlongfuird, the land of Drumlamford was owned in 1631 by John Campbell of Kinganecleuch but was acquired by the Kennedys of Kirkmichael. It was later sold and is described in great detail by James Paterson in the *History of the County of Ayr* (1847): 'It now, with other lands, forms the estate of Thomas Dickenson Rotch, Esq., who has been at great expense in improving them. His house, which was lately built, and of granite, stands surrounded by several mountain tarns, and to the south has Lochmaberry in view; while to the east and north it is surrounded by the magnificent mountain of Shallach-a-Minach, which is 2,700 feet above the sea. In its own peculiar style of beauty, Drumlongfuird is unrivalled in the county; and we can safely say that the lovers of wild scenery will be fully satisfied by paying it a visit, while the agriculturist or stock breeder will be delighted with a

survey of Mr Rotch's farm. Mr Rotch – third son of Benjamin Rotch, from Massachusetts, in America, the introducer of the southern whale fishery into Britain – married Miss Katherine Wason, and has one son and three daughters.' Drumlamford House was built near the western shore of Loch Dornal to the southeast of Barrhill in 1830–41 from Galloway granite and formed part of a large country estate that at one time had over 16,000 acres. The estate was owned in 1912 by Sir William Beale MP, who was created Baronet of Drumlamford, and is still owned by this family.

Black Clauchrie House was built to the northeast of Barrhill between 1898 and 1901 by James K. Hunter as a luxurious shooting lodge for the Austen family. The house occupies a sloping site and is in the Arts and Crafts style. The lodge has a large ballroom that was originally designed as the billiard room. The room has an inglenook fireplace, a high vaulted ceiling with exposed timbers, and a minstrel's gallery. There are also wood-panelled dining and drawing rooms, exposed wooden beams throughout the house, open fires in most rooms, a gun room, kennels, and a large glasshouse that overlooks the gardens and the Clauchrie Burn. Whereas in the past the house catered for large shooting parties, today it is run as a successful luxury self-catering holiday home and proves popular for weddings and small family celebrations with the ballroom now being used for ceilidhs.

The Established Arnsheen Church was built in 1887 by Robert Ingram in a Scottish baronial style just to the northwest of Barrhill on the man road to Girvan. The church was built on a small knoll overlooking a bend in the Duisk River, its tower rising 55 feet in height from the southeast corner; the manse is just visible on the right of this photograph from July 1929. Within the village of Barrhill a small path leads up the side of the Cross Water to a secluded spot in a wood where two graves have been carefully maintained by the inhabitants of the village. This is known as the Martyrs' Tomb Walk and the inscription on the tomb reads: 'Here lie John Murchie and Daniel M'Ilwrick, Martyrs, 1685.' These Covenanters were discovered at New Luce about twelve miles away and had been pursued by soldiers to the area and found hidden at the farmhouse of Alticannoch. Without any trial the men were taken from the house and searched. Bibles were found on them, which was seen as proof of their guilt, and they were shot. Two local women came by later at night and buried the dead men and in 1825 the present Martyrs' Monument was erected.

This is the magnificent west and southwest view of Kildonan House that was built to the northwest of Barrhill on the banks of the Duisk River within Kildonan Estate. The name is derived from the old medieval chapel that was dedicated to St Donan and which was once located within the estate's extensive grounds. Captain Euan Wallace MP had inherited 30,000 acres of land from his uncle on the condition that he would actually live there. James Miller, a Glasgow architect, was commissioned to design a large mansion house based on the Cotswold-style of architecture. Work commenced in 1915 and finished in 1923. The house had 65 rooms, indoor tennis courts and even a theatre, and was surrounded by beautiful landscaped gardens and rolling lawns. Captain Wallace lived there until his death in 1941 despite having to sell half of his land due to a shortage of capital. The house was then sold with the Sisters of St Joseph of Cluny converting it to a convent boarding school until 1976, when it was closed. In the early 1980s a proposal was put forward to turn the house and its surrounding land into a luxury holiday development with chalets but planning permission was refused and in 1988, after many years of lying empty, it was refurbished and converted into a luxury hotel with self-catering apartments.

Looking northwards along the main road between Newton Stewart to Girvan. The ruins of Pinwherry Castle are on the right, while in the centre of the photograph are the entrance gates and the long drive leading up to Pinwherry House, which is just out of view on the right. Far left can be seen the old toll house and the bridge carrying the main road over the Duisk River, while on its slightly elevated position is the schoolhouse. In 1880 the small school at Pinwherry had accommodation for 69 pupils and had an average attendance of 57 with grants of £47 3s. Pinwherry Castle dates from the late sixteenth century when it was built for John Kennedy of Banquharrie. The castle was erected here due to the strategic importance of the location – the confluence of the Stinchar and the Duisk, and the main highway that led from Newton Stewart to Girvan. The five-storey tower house was owned by the Kennedys until 1644 when it was sold to the Pollocks and then later abandoned sometime before the end of the eighteenth century.

Pinwherry Railway Station was opened on 5 October 1877 on the Glasgow & South Western railway line that ran from Girvan to Stranraer. This is the view looking southwards from the side of the railway banking where the line passes directly under the road leading from Pinwherry to Ballantrae. The stationmaster's house is next to the two platforms while just further down the line is the signal tower. According to locals the signalman at Pinwherry Station trained his dog to collect and return the hooped tablet from train drivers while he stayed in the signal box operating the levers. This photograph shows two tracks but the track on the left was used as the loop line to allow trains to pass safely, and also to give access into a small goods yard. In 1928 a freight train on its way to Girvan derailed into the field beyond the track after passing through the station at speed. On the left is the main road to Pinmore and Girvan and, on the hill beyond, Drumspillan House can be seen. The station closed on 6 September 1965.

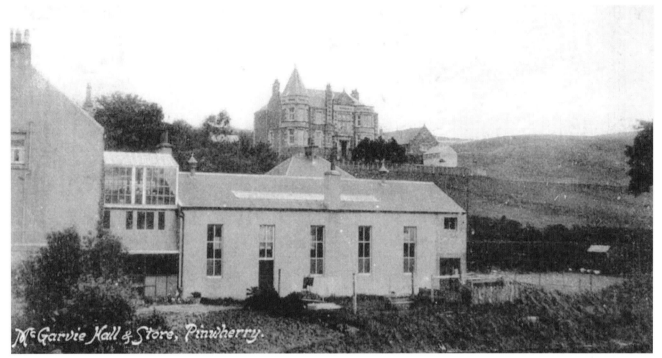

The McGarvie Hall and store at Pinwherry. The *Third Statistical Account*, published in 1951, reports that Pinwherry had 160 inhabitants with practically all the people employed on the surrounding farms; as a result the population was always in a constant state of flux as people arrived to get work during harvests or sheep-shearing times, leaving again when these were over. As well as the hall and store there was also a sub-post office. In the sixteenth century the two merklands of Pinquhirrie belonged to one of the numerous branches of the powerful Kennedys but it is uncertain as to whether it was that of Cassillis or Bargany. In 1688 the lands were acquired by John, Earl of Cassillis, and then subsequently by the Kennedys of Kirkhill and were sold by their descendant T.F. Kennedy of Dunure around the late 1830s to Mr Thomas Sloan. He was one of the most respectable farmers in the district and following his death in 1844 the lands of Pinquhirrie fell to his nephew, Mr Gilbert McClung. The village is named after nearby Pinwherry Hill which rises to a height of 548 feet.

A postman and his young assistant stand at the ornamental entrance gates to Alticane House near Pinwherry. The house takes its name from the nearby Alticane Burn which originates on Pinwherry Hill and cascades down through a wooded glen. Northeast from the house across the Duisk, on a commanding position high on the hill above Docherniel Farm, stands the prehistoric 'Glake' or 'Gleik Stane' as it is known locally. This is a spear shaped standing stone possibly dating from 2,000 BC. Docherniel Burn rises here and the name reputedly means the 'burn of the spear-shaped tombstone' while 'Glake' also means 'the ripple-shaped tombstone.' The standing stone has ancient cup-shaped and circular plate markings and is believed by archaeologists to have been used as an ancient calendar as, on midsummer's day, the shadow of the stone will point directly towards Knockdolian Hill.

Drumspillan House was designed and built in 1896 with beautiful landscaped gardens by the Glasgow architect James Lindsay. The *Carrick Herald* of 26 February 1926 reported on the destruction of the house: 'Disastrous fire at Pinwherry – Father and son burned to death – mansion house destroyed – A terrible conflagration occurred at Pinwherry at an early hour on Thursday morning. Drumspillan House being burned to the ground, and its owner, Mr Richard Whyte, and one of his sons, James Whyte, being burned to death. . . . The Ayr fire brigade arrived about five o'clock and although they did everything possible to save the building, their efforts proved unavailing and the valuable furniture and splendid fabric were completely destroyed, nothing now remaining but the gaunt outer walls. The fire raged for three hours and lit up the whole countryside. Mr Whyte purchased Drumspillan House about six years ago, and was deeply interested in bee culture, and exported large quantities of honey. His boy Derrick is being looked after by Mr and Mrs McKinnon, the Schoolhouse, Pinwherry.' The funeral procession passed through Girvan on its way to Cathcart Cemetery in Glasgow.

Hallowchapel Farm is located near Pinwherry at the junction of the main Girvan to Newton Stewart road with the minor road that branches off to Colmonell and Ballantrae. In the foreground is the River Stinchar and just further downstream is the confluence with the Duisk, the Stinchar's largest tributary. There were several old chapels or places of worship within the parish in past times and one of these, at this site although long gone, was dedicated to all saints and called Allhallow Chapel or Hallow Chapel. When churches were erected in the villages of Colmonell and Barrhill the chapel was no longer used and in recent years the name has become corrupted and it is now frequently called Hollowchapel. Visible in the background is the bulk of Pinwherry Hill.

Poundland is a small clachan of houses at the foot of the Poundland Burn on the banks of the River Stinchar, a mile west of Pinwherry and about two and a quarter miles northeast of Colmonell. A Reformed Presbyterian church and manse was erected here in the early nineteenth century and existed until 1898, when its congregation joined the Free Church in Colmonell. Poundland House was also built nearby on a slight hill overlooking the small hamlet. This is the view looking west along the main road.

Burnfoot Cottage overlooks the main road on the banks of the River Stinchar at Daljarrock, near Pinwherry. This was a turbulent place after the Reformation when Kennedy of Cassillis fought against Kennedy of Bargany. The Kennedys of Daljarrock were a branch of the Bargany family and in an incident at Pennyglen in December 1601 Alexander Kennedy of Daljarrock was involved in the murder of Richard Spens, servant to the Earl of Cassillis. This particular feud reached its climax near the end of 1601 when Bargany, a headstrong, aggressive young man, tried to ambush the Earl of Cassillis at Daljarrock. The plot was simple and easy to execute as Bargany and the Laird of Bennan would hide, concealed in an outhouse or limekiln at Daljarrock and shoot the Earl as he rode past on his way from the castle of Craigneil to his townhouse in Maybole. Cassillis heard of the plot in time to change his route but was enraged and vowed revenge. Only a week later Bargany rode openly through Cassillis' territory to Ayr accompanied by the men who had tried to murder the Earl at Daljarrock. Cassillis gathered a force and lay in wait to see if Bargany would dare to return by way of Maybole. However, Bargany learned of the danger and hired 80 armed men in Ayr and set out for home along the old High Road to Maybole in a snowstorm on 11 December. Cassillis met him at Ladycross, near Brockloch, and after some shouting, shots were fired and the Ayr men fled leaving Bargany at the mercy of his enemies. One of Bargany's former followers, now riding with Cassillis, struck Bargany in the throat with a lance and the feud was over. Bargany was carried away and died in Ayr some days later. Naturally uproar followed and Bargany's widow took the matter to the Privy Council in Edinburgh, but the decision was that Bargany had deliberately invaded Cassillis' territory and absolved the 'King of Carrick' from any blame.

According to Abercrombie, writing in 1696, Daljarrock House stood on the north side of the Stinchar, 'at the head of a pleasant plaine, looking westward, below which Stinchar receives Duisk'. It was the property of the Kennedys of Daljarrock and dates from around 1750, although there are indications an even earlier building may have occupied the site. Alterations and additions were undertaken in 1928 by the Glasgow architect Reginald Fairlie for the then owner, Major W.H. Coltman, but the house suffered from a disastrous fire in 1986 which resulted in the later Georgian alterations being demolished the following year. Daljarrock House was also once the home of Robert Kennedy, father-in-law of Gavin Hamilton, Robert Burns's friend and patron in Mauchline. While visiting the house Burns saw Kennedy's young daughter Peggie Kennedy and was so inspired by her beauty that she became the heroine of his poem 'Young Peggy'. This photograph shows the original house on the left with the large extension on the right. Today, it is run as a private hotel with the adjacent walled gardens being used as a small caravan park.

The Girvan to Stranraer railway opened on 5 October 1877 after five years of construction. It was operated by the Glasgow & South Western Railway Company and the line running south from Girvan had to negotiate the steep winding ascent from the Glendoune Bank all the way up past Laggan Hill before entering the 496-metre tunnel at Dinvin. Often trains would struggle on this climb and they could be heard for miles around puffing and screeching on the metal rails, especially when the weather was wet. At Holmhead, just south from Pinmore Station on a gentle curve spanning a small valley, is the railway's impressive eleven-arched Kinclaer Viaduct, also known as the Pinmore Viaduct. The chapel on the right was erected in 1878 by Allan Stevenson for Hugh Hamilton of Pinmore and within the kirkyard is a memorial to Captain Hugh Hamilton of nearby Pinmore House.

A view of Pinmore Station, showing the high signal tower, stationmaster's house and the single platform that was on the up line, while just out of picture on the left was a small goods yard. Two tracks can be seen but one was used as the loop line to allow approaching trains to pass in safety, although during the Second World War an accident occurred here. A goods train emerged from the nearby tunnel at a much higher speed than normal as another train was waiting at the platform. The goods train was swiftly diverted onto the goods line, which led directly into the yard where it ploughed into two stationary wagons and an empty coach. The wagons were smashed to pieces although luckily there were no casualties, with only the train driver suffering slight cuts and bruises. The station closed on 6 September 1965 and the stationmaster's house is now a private dwelling.

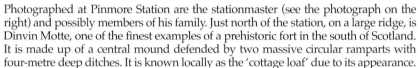

Photographed at Pinmore Station are the stationmaster (see the photograph on the right) and possibly members of his family. Just north of the station, on a large ridge, is Dinvin Motte, one of the finest examples of a prehistoric fort in the south of Scotland. It is made up of a central mound defended by two massive circular ramparts with four-metre deep ditches. It is known locally as the 'cottage loaf' due to its appearance.

The smartly dressed stationmaster of Pinmore Station. Many tales of the supernatural are associated with South Ayrshire and the ghostly apparition of a young woman was reputedly seen on the railway line near this station. In 1939 this ghostly figure was apparently seen throwing herself onto the rails under a passing train, much to the horror of those who witnessed it. The figure has also been seen standing by the side of the tracks.

Kilpatrick farmhouse stands on the gentle lower slopes of Daldowie Hill overlooking the River Stinchar just to the east of Asselfoot near Pinmore. A description of this area in the *Topographical Dictionary of Scotland* (1846) relates, 'The soil on the banks of the Stinchar is extremely fertile; the higher lands are chiefly a stiff clay, resting upon gravel, and a considerable portion is poor moorland, affording scanty pasturage. The chief crops are oats, wheat, barley, potatoes, and turnips; the system of agriculture is in a very advanced state, and all the more recent improvements are in general practice. Great attention is paid to the management of the dairy, and about 4,000 stone of cheese are annually produced for the neighbouring markets. The Cunninghame breed of cows is daily increasing, and about 500 of that kind are pastured on the several dairy-farms; the cattle reared are chiefly of the Galloway breed, and about 1,500 are annually sold to the cattle-dealers from the south. About 9,000 sheep of the black-faced breed, and 200 of the Cheviot and Leicestershire breeds, are annually pastured, on the average. The rateable annual value of the parish is £12,425. Limestone is extensively quarried, and there are five kilns, at which about 20,000 bolls of lime are burnt for manure every year. Salmon is also found in the River Stinchar; and there are several salmon pools, the rents of which, in the aggregate, amount to £30 per annum.'

A horsedrawn carriage on the main road near Pinmore gatehouse in the early 1900s. The gatehouse was at the entrance to Pinmore Estate, owned by the Hamilton family, and within this, situated close to the Pinmore Viaduct, was Assel Mill. It was originally a corn and meal mill but was later converted into a sawmill with the dam being close to the road at Kinclear. There was also an old mill on the River Stinchar at Pinclanty while further downstream was Almont Mill. The mill was fitted with three pairs of millstones for oatmeal, shelling oats and for cattle provender and was three floors in height. In 1893 a large tree was blown down at Pinmore House during a bad storm and following heavy rain and severe flooding was carried away downstream by the River Stinchar. The tree struck the dam for the mill with

such force that it left a chasm over 64 feet in length. Afterwards repair work was thwarted when the river rose again and carried away the skeleton dam that was being constructed. Iron rails were later used to help strengthen the dam but the force of the water was such that these became bent and the mill dam was breached again.

Pinmore Castle was built and added to throughout the sixteenth and seventeenth centuries and was located near Pinmore Railway Station on rising ground, overlooking what was often described as being one of the loveliest bends on the River Stinchar. It was long owned by the Hamilton family and was almost completely destroyed by fire in 1876. However, its then owner, Hugh Hamilton Esq., completely rebuilt and restored it the following year in a similar style of architecture, and it was also extended to plans by Allan Stevenson. Hugh Hamilton of Pinmore was responsible for erecting a bridge over the River Stinchar about halfway between Pinmore and Daljarrock, work beginning in April 1801. An oval stone in the centre of the bridge is engraved with the following, 'This bridge was erected by Hugh Hamilton of Pinmore in the year of our Lord 1802.', although it should be noted that he had received a grant of £257 from the Ayrshire Road Trustees to erect the bridge. His son, also called Hugh Hamilton, was a wealthy landowner holding 8,441 acres of land within the district, which was valued at £3,833 per annum in 1885. Pinmore House was again gutted by fire and eventually demolished in May 1982. A modern house now occupies the site.

A photograph taken from the flat-lying land near the south bank of the Water of Gregg and looking north to the village of Barr, taken in September 1929. On the left are the distinctive red tiles and timber gables of the Carnegie Morton Library, with the old cemetery and its stone arched entrance adjacent. To the right of this is the row of two storey houses, built in the early 1800s, where smoke can be seen coming from the chimney of the Jolly Shepherd. The Free Church on The Avenue is in the background.

Looking up Barr's Hill Street (now known as Glenginnet Road) from the junction with the Stinchar and Changue roads, September 1929. The post office was located on this street and there was also a small shop, seen on the right. The corner of the King's Arms Hotel (formerly the Albert Arms) is on the left while further up the road a pavement petrol pump is also visible. Just past the large tree is the junction for The Avenue. The Ayrshire Trade Directory of 1837 records that James McCaa was the postmaster with letters from Girvan arriving every Monday, Wednesday and Friday morning at half past ten, while mail from the village was despatched in the afternoon of the same days at two. In 1837 Barr had a parochial schoolhouse and also a small subscription library with a collection of nearly 200 books; Stephen Walker was both the master of the school and the librarian. The school was described as being 'well conducted' with the master's yearly salary being £34, 4 shillings and 4½ pennies, with £18 fees and an accompanying house and a garden.

In the foreground of this photograph is the fast flowing Water of Gregg and just out of picture on the left is the Gregg Bridge, which carries the main road south to Pinwherry or northwards to Old Dailly. The parish church, visible on the left, was built in 1878 by Allan Stevenson in early Gothic style, and paid for by Mr Griffin, an auditor from Edinburgh. It was constructed of whinstone cut from the bed of the River Stinchar and allowed for a congregation of 410 persons; a buttressed belfry was later added. The minister's annual stipend in 1846 was £231, three shillings and a penny. Also visible is the junction of Glebe Road while the Angus Memorial Free Church built by Alexander Petrie can be seen on its elevated position on The Avenue overlooking the village. It was built from red sandstone in 1891 with its spire being added in 1894 at a cost of £1,400. Three years later the clock was placed in the tower to celebrate the Diamond Jubilee of Queen Victoria. The grassy area on the right of this photograph, adjacent the old walled cemetery, was to become the site of the Carnegie Morton Library which opened in 1913 and is now known as the Village Institute. Apart from that, little has since changed in this scene; the parish church is still in regular use and the Free Church was recently restored and is now a private house.

The opening day of the Carnegie Morton Library, 4 April 1913.

Looking northwest along the Changue Road towards the King's Arms Hotel. In the *Ayrshire Trade Directory* published by Pigot and Co. in 1837, Barr was described as being, 'A small neat village, lying on the banks of the Rivers Gregg and Stinchar'. This directory records that William Harrison and John Thompson were carriers to Ayr every Friday and John Cowleson every alternate Tuesday. Matthew Dickie carried to Glasgow every alternate Tuesday, however mention is also made that little business was conducted with the surrounding district due to the lack of good roads.

The cottages of Windy Row are located just off Glenginnet Road and were aptly named due to their exposed location to the prevailing winds high on the hillside. In *A Topographical Dictionary of Scotland*, published in 1846, Barr Parish was described as having 959 inhabitants of whom only about 230 lived within the village. The parish comprised nearly 70,000 acres of land of which only 1,200 were arable and not more than 1,000 were capable of producing a profit. The soil in the lower lands was described as being of fair quality but that on the higher ground was mostly moss despite frequent surface draining. The main dependence therefore was on the rearing of cattle and sheep for which the moorland terrain proved adequate and the annual rateable value of the parish in 1846 was £7,578. The chief landed proprietors of the entire district at that time were the Marquis of Ailsa and Sir James Ferguson. Some of the shopkeepers and traders in the village were William Baird, surgeon; John Caldwell, blacksmith; William Ferguson, grocer and spirit dealer; George and John Forsyth, boot and shoe makers; George Gibb, shopkeeper and teacher; John McMurtrie, innkeeper; and Robert McCracken, blacksmith.

Looking upstream on the River Stinchar towards the humpbacked Stinchar Bridge that was built in 1787 to carry the main road from Girvan to Barr. The telegraph poles on the left mark the side of the main road as it leaves Barr and climbs steadily along the side of Auchensoul Hill where there are a number of sharp twists and bends known locally as 'The Screws'. Just south from the bridge was Alton Albany House, while further south on the banks of the river at Kirkland Hill are the remains of the old chapel of Kirkdominae where the celebrated local fair of Kirkdandie was held annually on the last Saturday of May until the late 1800s. Merchants and pedlars once travelled from all over Britain and Ireland to attend and sell their wares, however it often eventually disintegrated into a drunken brawl with much thieving and was no longer held.

Alton Albany was built in the 1830s on a position just off the main road to the south of Barr. The house was named after the nearby Albany Burn, which flows off the surrounding hills. It was extended in 1861 by the architect John Murdoch for Sir Geoffrey Henry Hughes-Onslow of Balkissock, a commander in the Royal Navy. In this photograph from the early 1900s the small bell that was once mounted on the roof is clearly visible. In recent years the house has been extensively restored and has a walled garden and lodge house.

Just south from Old Dailly, and surrounded by mature woodland on the edge of the Penwhapple Glen, is Penkill Castle, one of Ayrshire's finest castles and pictured here around 1907. A letter from Mr William Bell Scott, dating from the latter part of the nineteenth century, states: 'The oldest part of Penkill Castle, a high square block, with quoin-turrets, and an enclosing wall and gate, was built by Adam Boyd, whose tombstone stands in Old Dailly Churchyard, sometime in the sixteenth century; a newer and more commodious portion was added by Thomas Boyd, in 1628, as shown by various dates still existing; while the castle in its present state was the work of the late Spencer Boyd, who also lies now in the family burying place.' The castle was in a ruinous condition until inherited and restored by Spencer Boyd in 1857. The pre-Raphaelite poets and artists such as William Bell Scott, Dante Gabriel Rossetti, William Morris and Christina Rossetti frequently visited Penkill and the interior of the castle is decorated with many fine colourful murals painted by Scott, such as scenes from the 'King's Quair' which run around the spiral staircase.

Killochan Castle stands on the banks of the Water of Girvan just north of Old Dailly. It was built in 1586 by the Cathcarts and is a tall tower with a spiral staircase at one corner to which all the apartments are connected. Above the door to the castle, the words 'This work was begun the 1 of Marche 1586 be Johne Cathcart of Carlton and Helene Wallace his spous' are inscribed. The Cathcarts were once one of the most powerful families in Ayrshire and held a charter granted by King Robert the Bruce around 1324. Robert Cathcart of Killochan was killed at the Battle of Flodden in 1513. Within sight of the castle, in a grassy field that gently slopes down to the Water of Girvan, stands a huge boulder of grey granite weighing about 37 tons with a circumference of thirteen yards. This is the Baron's Stone and in former times formed the 'Hill of Justice' of the Killochan lairds. They would muster all their men here, plan their raids, share their booty and also execute any prisoners. Geologists believe the massive stone once formed part of a cliff near Loch Doon and was carried here by a glacier. Killochan Castle was occupied by the Cathcarts until 1954 and this photograph dating from the early 1900s shows the two-storey wing that was added in the eighteenth century. The castle is still a private residence.

This is the magnificent front view of Bargany Mansion House which is located to the west of Dailly overlooking the Water of Girvan. The Kennedys were the ancient lairds of Bargany but they were spendthrift and their lands were soon broken up and sold. In 1625 they were purchased by Sir John Hamilton, natural son of the first Marquis of Hamilton, who later received the title of Lord Bargany. The mansion house was built in 1681 by the second Lord Bargany and incorporated decorative stonework from the ruins of the original sixteenth-century Kennedy tower house that stood nearby. In 1747 the entrance was moved to the northeast side when the house was being redesigned but it was later returned to the southeast, its original location, when the house was further extended in 1845/46 by the architect William Burn. In the 1970s the house was abandoned and its condition deteriorated badly with its owner, Captain North Dalrymple-Hamilton, lodging an application with the local council in 1980 to have it demolished. This was refused and in 1985 the house and a few acres of surrounding parkland were purchased privately with the building being restored to its former condition by architect Patrick Lorimer in 1988–91. The extensive wooded grounds of the estate still remain the property of the Dalrymple-Hamilton family.

The attractive walled gardens and glasshouse at Bargany House, pictured around 1905. In January 1884, a terrific storm raged unabated for over three weeks, finally culminating near the end of the month in one of the most violent hurricanes and snowstorms that had ever been experienced in the British Isles. As the *Kilmarnock Standard* reported: 'Whipped up from the Atlantic, the gale caused incredible havoc in Ireland and England before its full force was felt in Scotland. Accompanying the storm was a heavy snowfall followed by a keen frost and from a meteorological point of view, the storm was the most remarkable to have occurred since the barometer was invented to mark the fluctuations of the atmosphere. The reading reaching its lowest level ever recorded in Scotland. The destruction was tremendous with damage being reported in every single town and village throughout Ayrshire. The noise of the storm was at times equal to that of the loudest thunder and few people found it possible to sleep. Many remained up all night in momentary expectation of some serious catastrophe but happily there was no loss of life and only injuries of a trifling nature were reported. The uprooting and damage of trees was enormous and on the extensive estate of Bargany, the property of the Countess of Stair, it was estimated that the number of trees blown down was around 100,000, with whole plantations being affected including some of the finest timber. The number of fallen trees was simply beyond calculation and included many rare species some of which were many hundreds of years old and irreplaceable. The widespread destruction from the great storm that had swept so powerfully over Ayrshire on that January night ensured that those who had experienced it would not readily forget it!' The extensive gardens at Bargany are open to the public throughout the summer months and contain a colourful display of azaleas and rhododendrons as well as a small lochan and pleasant woodland walks such as through the Weaver's Glen.

*Opposite*: One of the small cottages within the extensive Bargany Estate. Across the Girvan Water from the mansion house is the gently sloping grass of the 'Butler's Brae', where a small stone cottage once stood that was occupied by the butlers of Bargany. Two poets were born within this cottage. The first was Hamilton Paul, born on 10 April 1773, who became an occasional verse-maker, assistant editor of the *Ayr Advertiser* and eventually minister at Broughton in Peeblesshire, where he is buried within the churchyard. The second poet was born on 5 April 1792, the son of George Ainslie who was the butler at Bargany and who frequently looked after the house and estate when the laird was away from home on business. Often nicknamed the Carrick Bard, Hew Ainslie was a tall and slender man who humorously dubbed himself 'The Lang Linker' in one of his early volumes. He worked as assistant nurseryman on Bargany Grounds but at the age of seventeen moved with his father to Roslin where he found employment as a clerk in the Register Office in Edinburgh. In 1822 he emigrated to America and tried farming, brewing and building without much success and died in Louisville in 1878. The centenary of his birth was much celebrated within Girvan where a number of his songs were sung and his 'The Rover of Loch Ryan' is often regarded as one of the best Scottish sea songs ever written. The stone cottage where the poets were born was removed around the early 1840s.

Dailly Parish Church, built in 1776, is at least the third that has existed within the parish. The first stood somewhere near Kilkerran, the second at Old Dailly, and this one forms the centre of 'New' Dailly. Until recent times, it was known as St Machar's Church after St Machar who founded a small chapel in the first century near Machrikill to the south of the village. A new pulpit was erected in 1893 and twelve standard lamps were installed in 1894, fed by oil. Between 1913 and 1915 the building was given a new roof and the south gable was rebuilt with the Bargany aisle lengthened by ten feet and lit by a new tall window. Gas Lighting was also installed along with a new asphalt floor, pulpit and new pine pews. The church overlooks a small square and the distinctive war memorial, designed by James A. Morris, which was erected in 1922 to honour those that had fallen in the Great War. In the small graveyard of the church are a number of interesting tombstones marking the resting places of village worthies of former days and some of the ministers who had served the parish, and a mausoleum to the Lairds of Kilkerran, the Fergusson family who were created Baronets of Kilkerran in 1703 and who owned the land on which the village stood. One of the most notable tombstones is that in memory of John Brown, collier, who in 1835 was trapped in Kilgrammie Coal Pit on the estate of Bargany, when part of the workings collapsed. He was eventually rescued, still alive, albeit in a very exhausted state, after surviving without food and being in the cold and pitch darkness for some 23 days. He lived for three days before succumbing to his ordeal at the age of 66 years.

Looking east along Dailly's Main Street towards the parish church. On the right children can be seen standing outside the entrance gate to the village community centre which was built in 1906 by the Girvan Hall Company; in 1916 the building was acquired by the Coal Industry Employees who built a new frontage in 1920. It became known as the Working Men's Club Rooms but was informally called the 'Club Room'. Inside it had a main hall with a small stage, two reading rooms, a snooker room and living accommodation for the caretaker. The *New Statistical Account* of 1837 recounted of Dailly: 'There is only one village in the parish; it has been greatly enlarged within the last twelve years. All the new houses are built substantially and in regular order. An arrangement was made, fourteen years ago, under the sanction of the General Post Office, by which the letters for the village were brought everyday from the post town, Maybole; and for the last five years a branch post office from Maybole has been regularly established.' The post office can be seen just to the right of the church at the end of the street. It closed in January 2009 and post office facilities are now within a local store. The last postmistress was Barbara Campbell.

Looking west along the Main Street towards the cottages at West End. Two horsedrawn carts are carrying their heavy load of timber into the sawmill owned by Wilson and Sons that is just visible on the right behind the two single-storey cottages. The sawmill was a three-storey building and originally contained four pairs of millstones for shelling oats and smutting wheat. Power was obtained from the large dam that stretched from the north bank of the Water of Girvan to the sluice that ran along the rear of the houses on Main Street to reach the large wooden breast paddle wheel at the mill. In 1855/56 James Dunlop was recorded as the miller and tenant of the mill, and by 1880 it had ceased to produce flour and cattle provender and was used solely as a sawmill. In 1883/84 the new tenants were Messrs Adam Wilson and his sons William, Gilbert, David and James, who were described as saw millers employed in the manufacture of timber from the extensive wooded policies on the Dalquharran and Bargany Estates. Today, little remains of the mill and the deep lade that ran along the rear of the houses has been filled in to become a public park. By the time of this photograph the miller was William S. Fettes who retired in 1939 after working at the mill for over thirty years cutting timber. The mill closed when he retired. Across the street is the Central Bar which is still open today.

Looking further west along the Main Street, the King's Arms Hotel is visible on the left followed by the junction for Bridge Street, while directly opposite the sharp turn to the right leads to the stone bridge over the Water of Girvan. The hotel is now closed and the building is in a ruinous state with no roof. The cottages visible on the left with the bicycle parked at the side, at the corner of Bridge Street and West End, were later demolished and a Miner's Memorial was erected in 1999 to commemorate mining in the area. The plaque on it reads 'Dedicated to the miners of the Girvan Valley Coalfield 1415–1977', and it marks the former meeting place of local miners who would gather here either prior to the start of their shifts or on days off to engage in chat regarding local affairs. The monument is in the form of a large boulder of rock and there are also two metal benches decorated with carvings of mining memorabilia.

Bridge Street climbs steeply up from its junction with Main Street and takes its name from the Dailly Bridge over the Water of Girvan. The cottages here were likely at some point to have housed mining families. The New Statistical Account of 1837 relates that, 'The parish abounds in . . . coal, limestone, and sandstone (freestone). The form or shape of the coalfield is that of a long elliptical basin, extending about six miles in a northeast and southwest line of bearing through the parish. Its breadth is about 600 yards. Eminent engineers consider it as forming part of the great coalfield which stretches across the island from the neighbourhood of Edinburgh, in a southwesterly direction, into Ayrshire. The coalfield here consists of five workable seams of coal, varying in thickness from four to fourteen feet, and cropping out to the surface on both sides of the basin. . . . The seams are all of good quality, but are subject to various dislocations. . . . The coal is worked to considerable extent on the estates of Bargany and Dalquharran. Steam engines have been employed at both collieries for a number of years. The sales are principally for home consumption; but coals are also shipped from these collieries to Ireland and elsewhere. The gas which is used at Ayr is obtained from the Dalquharran parrot coal. The sales may amount annually to 20,000 tons. The cost of a ton at the pit head is about 4s.8d or 5s. A ton weighs 24 cwt., and there are eight creels in a ton.'

The Lindsayton Burn flows off the surrounding hills to the southeast of Dailly and passes under the Upper Roan Bridge and then under the main road at the Roan Bridge. The New Statistical Account noted that 'The parish is well supplied with roads; on the north side of the valley, one turnpike road extends about five miles; another runs through the valley, and along the south side, about six miles and a half. From these, three other turnpike roads branch off to the right and left for a mile or two. A coach passes and repasses through the parish on Friday, on its route between Girvan and Ayr. There are three public bridges and one private bridge across the Girvan; and there are a number of other bridges across smaller streams. Some of them have been erected at great expense, for the sake of the new lines of road which were lately formed. All at present in good condition, and from the attention paid to the state of the roads, are likely to be kept in thorough repair.' This view from 1905 is looking upstream as the burn winds its way under the main road from Crosshill as it enters the village.

A view looking down Greenhead Street towards Main Street. Greenhead Street connected Main Street with Back Road, which ran almost parallel and a large nursery with several glasshouses were located on it as well as the former United Free Church which closed in 1938. There was also a number of small cottages, the schoolhouse and a newer school building, and some of the council houses that were built in the years after 1920. There was a major shortage of housing within the village at that time and 60 houses were built in total by the council to alleviate this. One hundred and sixty miners and their families lived in Dailly but over 100 other men travelled from Girvan or from the miner's rows at Kilgrammie and Wallacetown as they could not reside with their families within the village due to the severe shortage of housing. The miners were entitled to free coal but this was frequently just tipped onto the street outside their house and men shovelling the coal into barrows and pails was a common sight. At the bottom of the street a bus is parked in front of the branch of the Royal Bank Of Scotland, while adjacent in the narrow lane were the premises of Coleman the electrician.

Just to the north of Dailly was Lochmodie Toll, which was frequently spelt as 'Lochmoddy' or 'Lochmuddie' Toll. The name derives from the remains of Lochmodie Castle which once stood by the side of the Quarrel Hill Burn. The fast-flowing stream tumbles down off the surrounding hills and runs under the main road and in this scene dating from the early 1900s, a young boy is sitting on the Lochmodie Bridge. Just beyond the bridge is the toll house that once stood at the junction of the main turnpike road from Dailly to Girvan while visible further along the road, on the right, are the entrance gates to the extensive policies of the Dalquharran Castle that was completed in 1790. Travellers on this road would pass through Dalquharran Mains and Wallacetown on their way to Maybole and for most of their journey on the narrow, twisting road would overlook the railway line that ran from Ayr, via Maybole to Girvan. A small station opened near Lochmodie in 1869 for travellers to Dailly although this has since closed. The toll house was abandoned and demolished in the early 1960s.

Looking upstream on the Water of Girvan as it flows past Dailly manse and over the stone dam that stretched from the north bank across the river to the intake just out of view on the right. Partly hidden by trees, the manse was built in 1801 just off Linfern Road and was occupied by the ministers of the parish church on Main Street. One of the most famous ministers to occupy the pulpit was the Reverend John Thompson. The youngest of eight children, he was born in Dailly on 1 September 1778, the fourth son of the local parish minister. Inspired by the beautiful Ayrshire countryside, John displayed an amazing talent for sketching and painting from an early age and enrolled at Glasgow University in 1791 to study law and theology and two years later transferred to Edinburgh University to further his studies for the ministry. There he met Sir Walter Scott and was given art lessons by Alexander Nasmyth, and after graduating John returned to Dailly in 1800 to become minister. Thomson became a renowned landscape artist with an established reputation and moved to Duddingston near Edinburgh to become the parish minister; he also had his own studio there. He became friends with many distinguished people, including the writer Sir Thomas Dick Lauder, and died in October 1840 having spent 41 years in the ministry.

The history of the estate of Dalquharran can be traced as far back as the early fourteenth century and standing on a small knoll on the banks of a sweeping bend of the Water of Girvan near Dailly are the extensive ruins of Dalquharran Castle. Now known as old Dalquharran Castle and dating from the fifteenth century, the keep was built by the Kennedys of Culzean. It was three storeys in height, with a large round tower at one corner with a corbelled-out parapet and a vaulted ground floor, and was considerably extended in the late seventeenth century. Along with the estate of Dalquharran, it was purchased soon after by Sir Thomas Kennedy of Kirkhill, Lord Provost of Edinburgh. The castle remained inhabited until sometime around 1790 when it was finally abandoned for the new mansion, also called Dalquharran Castle and visible here in the background, which was built on a more commanding position.

The new castle at Dalquharran was built between 1785 and 1790 by the renowned Scottish architect Robert Adam on an elevated site overlooking the Water of Girvan. It was built for Thomas Kennedy of Dunure who had just married Adam's niece and the castle was described as being as magnificent as Culzean Castle, with even more elaborate interior furnishings. In 1880 the castle was considerably extended with large wings being added to both the northwest and southeast sides, but this work left the family almost bankrupt. The Kennedy family moved elsewhere and the castle and its grounds were leased as a private hunting and fishing estate. Soon it was put up for auction and bought by a timber merchant from Troon who set about stripping the timber from the estate and in 1936 the castle was leased to the Scottish Youth Hostel Association (as seen here). It remained a youth hostel until the Second World War when the Langside School for the deaf, evacuated from Glasgow, moved in. During the war the castle and its lands were sold to John Stewart, a produce merchant from Girvan, who moved in with his family and friends. He farmed the estate but the castle proved too large and expensive to maintain and in 1967 it was finally abandoned with the lead on the roof being removed to save paying excessive taxes. The impressive shell of Dalquharran Castle still overlooks the village of Dailly and there are ambitious plans to turn it into a luxury hotel and transform the grounds into an exclusive golf course.

Dalquharran School at Wallacetown near Dailly, photographed around 1906. Schools were frequently built by the wealthy estate owners to educate their workers and this was one such school. Coal was worked to a considerable extent from the pit on Dalquharran Estate and in 1896 the estate employed some 94 underground and 22 surface workers at the pit, while many found employment on the extensive estate planting and cutting the timber or within the castle itself as servants and maids. The school was closed around 1926 and the building is now awaiting renovation. The small thatched cottage next to it was a shop and post office and the post box can still be seen on one of its walls.

Kilkerran House is located within the extensive Kilkerran Estate that lies between Crosshill and Dailly. It was built around 1730 for Sir James Ferguson, Lord Kilkerran, on the site of the old tower of Barclanachan, which may also have been incorporated into the house. The mansion was remodelled by William Adam and extended further in 1818 by James Gillespie Graham, in 1854 by David Bryce, and again in 1873. A large monument on Kildoon Hill near Maybole erected in 1853 commemorates Sir Charles D. Ferguson of Kilkerran (1800–1849) who was responsible for building Maybole's West Church and Crosshill Church and who provided funds to many of the local schools and charities in the district. The mansion stands in a pleasant location with the woodlands behind and the large open grassland park at the front. Two miles southwest, at Lindsayston Glen, are the remains of the fifteenth-century keep that was the original Kilkerran Castle and was a Ferguson stronghold and it was from here that the Fergusons relocated. This view shows the rear of the house and the beautiful landscaped gardens. Kilkerran House suffered a fire in April 1994 but has since been extensively restored.

Workers in the gardens of Kilkerran House.

Photographed in 1929, this is the rustic stone bridge crossing the Lady Burn in Kilkerran Estate's Lady Glen. Both are named after the ruins of the Lady Chapel to the Virgin Mary which can be found within the glen. In his *Views of Carrick*, the Rev. R. Lawson noted of Kilkerran Estate, 'Its grounds are famous for their beauty. In particular, the Lady Glen is a gem of beauty, and should be visited by every person who comes to Carrick. The trees of Kilkerran, too, are famed, and the magnificent beech by the entrance drive, as well as the silver firs of the Lady Glen (over 100 feet high), are admired by all lovers of forestry.'

Ladyburn is located at the eastern end of the extensive Kilkerran Estate near Crosshill. This was once the dower house of the Fergusons of Kilkerran and was named after the nearby Lady Burn that flows down off Cairn Hill. The house has been recently used as a private hotel.

*Above*: Looking south towards Crosshill in July 1929. The main road from Maybole can be seen crossing the Water of Girvan at the Crosshill Bridge before entering into King Street. The United Free Church, just off Newton Street, is visible within the village itself (centre right) while toward the left, standing prominently alone, is the parish church and manse with the public school and houses on the Kirkmichael Road behind it. Just beyond the village, behind and to the right of the United Free Church, on the road that leads to the crossroads at Cloyntie and ringed by trees, is Dalhowan. It was here in the early 1800s that the original proprietor had the foresight to commence feuing on his land and this led directly to the establishment of the village itself. In the immediate foreground (just out of view) is the single-track road that leads to Dalcur and Dalduff where the remains of an ancient sixteenth-century castle can still be seen today at Dalduff Farm.

*Below*: Looking west towards Crosshill in the early 1930s, with the parish church of 1853 dominating the foreground. Just behind the church are the then-new council houses built along Milton Street, while on the far left the main road to Dailly can be seen winding its way towards Kileekie. The football pitch on the Recreation Ground is on the right, while further to the right and just out of view is the bridge carrying the main road to Maybole over the Water of Girvan – this part of the village is known as Brigend. In the glory days of amateur football Crosshill Thistle were very successful, winning the Ayrshire Cup in the 1958/59 season and the Sir Thomas Moore Trophy four times in a five-year spell between 1959/60 and 1963/64. They also won the James Howie Cup in season 1960/61. Former Rangers and Scotland captain George Young was the invited special guest at the club's annual end of season social in 1959 when they won the Ayrshire Cup.

Crosshill's King Street, looking towards Brigend from the Cross in July 1929. The war memorial on the right stands at the junction of Newton Street, while just off to the left the main road leads up past Kileekie to Dailly. Many of the single-storey handloom cottages were built either side of the principal street by the original occupants of the village who were predominantly Irish or from Irish descendants. In the early 1880s George McMichael wrote in his book *Notes on the Way Through Ayrshire* that 'The village of Crosshill is built on the left side of Girvan Water, crossed here by a bridge, two miles southwest of Kirkmichael. It is a bright looking place, with shops, a post office (with money order and savings bank departments), established and Free churches, public schools, various blacksmiths' and joiners' shops, and a grain mill.'

Looking southeast from the Brigend along King Street towards the Cross in the early 1900s. In the 1830s there were a number of traders and craftsmen who lived and worked within the village including John Blair, surgeon, and James Cooper, Robert King, Alexander McCulloch and Joseph McCulloch, all innkeepers and vintners. Agnes Andrew operated a small grocer's shop and was also the village postmistress with letters arriving from Maybole every morning at eight and being despatched every afternoon at five. Other traders were William Cook, tailor, James Cooper, grocer, John Craig, shoemaker, John Goudie, blacksmith, John McClure, agent for the Glasgow cotton manufacturers, and David McHutchinson, grocer and another agent for the Glasgow cotton manufacturers. In the foreground of the photograph can be seen one of the metal street wells that were used to obtain fresh water prior to the installation of a piped water supply to the village.

Looking eastwards from the Cross into Newton Street. On the right is the bell tower of the United Free Church while in the distance can be seen the manse for the parish church. On the left are some of the original single-storey handloom cottages. A local trader, possibly from Maybole, with his horse and cart can be seen travelling along the street. Traders from Maybole were a common sight as they made frequent country runs to villages such as Crosshill, Kirkmichael and Straiton where they sold everything from general goods, bakery, fresh fish and meat, and ironmongery. The war memorial, in the form of a large monolith, was publicly unveiled on 9 April 1921 at a special ceremony where hymns were sung and an address was given by the Marquis of Ailsa, Lord Lieutenant of the county. To mark the conclusion of the ceremony the national anthem was sung with music being provided by a brass band, and a small booklet was also given to those in attendance. The monument was inscribed with the names of 24 local men. The memorial was later inscribed with the names of the five local men who died during the Second World War.

Looking southwards from the Cross up the gentle slope into Dalhowan Street around 1915. On the left is the junction of Newton Street which led to the Free Church while on the right is the junction for the Dailly road over the Manse Bridge and Kileekie. Also on the right at No. 2 Dalhowan Street is the Crosshill Arms Inn, later known as the Crosshill Arms Hotel, while the gable advertising for the Plough Inn can also be seen at the foot of the Kirkmichael Road. On the left a number of children are standing outside one of the small shops that existed within Crosshill at this time. A trade directory for Maybole published around 1950 listed within the village a baker, blacksmith, boot and shoe maker, a draper, four general grocers, a spirit dealer, a tailor and clothiers, and also the 'fully licensed' Royal Hotel which was located in King Street. The Crosshill Arms Hotel still trades today.

Looking north along Dalhowan Street towards the Cross. The street took its name from the original estate of Dalhowan. The *New Statistical Account* recounts that, 'The former proprietor of Crosshill built a large schoolhouse for the benefit of the village. There is a small salary paid by the feuars to the master, amounting at present to L.3, 10s. The school has been lately connected with the General Assembly's scheme. The average attendance is about 70. From the poverty of the inhabitants, the payment of the school wages is wretched in the extreme.' There was also a Sabbath school for children and young communicants with an attendance of 130. The school was located near the top of the Kirkmichael Road but a new school for primary education was built in 1968 just off Carrick Drive. This scene has changed little; even the metal water pumps remain.

Looking east up the gentle slope of the Kirkmichael Road in Crosshill that leads to the nearby village of Kirkmichael. On the left are some of the original stone cottages and on the right is the junction of Back Street. At the top of the road was the manse, the public school and there was also once a well. The village of Crosshill was originally just one long main street roughly a quarter of a mile in length with the Kirkmichael Road being the only other street branching off from this. This scene has now changed considerably as modern houses were built at Kirkbride Crescent and Carrick Drive branching off from the street, and the bowling green is also now situated at the top of the Kirkmichael Road.

To the south of Crosshill is Kirkbride House, formerly known as Glenmoor House and built in 1861 on an elevated position atop a small hill by Sir Thomas Montgomery Cunninghame. His son, William James Montgomery Cunninghame, served as a lieutenant with the 1st Battalion Rifle Brigade (Prince Consort's Own) during the Crimean War. For his bravery in action he was awarded the Victoria Cross on 26 June 1857 in Hyde Park, London, by Queen Victoria herself. Cunninghame attained the rank of colonel and, while still serving, his wife and children lived at Kirkbride House (it was he who had decided to rename the house). He retired from the army after 24 years service and served as a Tory MP for Ayr from 1874 to 1880. He died on 11 November 1897 and was buried in the family plot in Kirkmichael Churchyard. Kirkbride House was sold to the Houldsworth family in 1916 and was extended in 1924, but most of the alterations were later removed. This photograph dates from around 1910.

This photograph from July 1929 shows the small natural lake that is located within the Kirkbride Estate. On the left along the base of the trees is the road that south from Crosshill to Balloch, going over the moors along the Nick of Balloch to Newton Stewart. The cottage at the side of the road marks the entrance into Kirkbride House and still stands today.

To the south of Straiton stands Balbeg House. Originally built as a simple farmhouse in the nineteenth century, it was extended in 1908 by Sir Charles Fergusson of Kilkerran and in 1923 by Sir Gerald Healey to become a substantial shooting lodge. The name is taken from the Balbeg Burn that flows off the surrounding bleak moorland hills and past the house on its way to join the Water of Girvan.

Looking east along Straiton's Main Street, towards the entrance gates of Traboyack Manse where the road takes a sharp turn to the right before ascending on its way to Newton Stewart. On both sides of Main Street are the distinctive rows of handloom weavers cottages, some still with their thatched roofs, built by Thomas, Earl of Cassillis, in the 1760s. Dominating the background is the towering bulk of Craigengower Hill and the large granite obelisk that was erected in 1856 to honour the memory of Colonel James Hunter Blair MP of Blairquhan who was killed in 1854 at the Battle of Inkerman during the Crimean War. On the right is the sign for the Black Bull Inn which dates from 1766 and which famously featured in a national television advert for Tennent's Lager in the early 1970s. Straiton also became the fictional Highland village of Inverdoune in the 1999 film, *The Match*, which starred Richard E. Grant.

Milton House is located just off the main road from Ayr, prior to entering the village of Straiton. This is the Dower House of Blairquhan Estate and was built around 1885 by Sir Edward Hunter Blair, fourth baronet. The house has a beautiful location overlooking the Water of Girvan as it slowly winds its way through the wooded policies of the estate. Milton was where David Hunter Blair lived, at the age of 22, after he succeeded to the baronetcy following the death of his older brother. He disliked the old castle at Blairquhan, preferring to house his estate workers there. However, on a visit to Edinburgh in 1813 he fell in love and married Dorothea Hay McKenzie, niece of the Marquis of Tweeddale. He consulted with several prominent architects to redesign the old castle for himself, his wife and their three young children, but sadly Dorothea died in 1820. However, Sir David devoted all his energies into working with the architect William Burn to design and build a magnificent home for his children. The old castle was dismantled and a new castle built, incorporating decorative stonework from the old, and in the years during its construction Sir David and his children lived at Milton.

This was the result of Blair and Burn's work, built between 1821 and 1824. It replaced the earlier castle of 1575 that itself had incorporated parts of an old tower house dating from the fourteenth century. The land was originally the property of the MacWhurters, but passed to the Kennedys during the fifteenth century and then to the Whitefoords of Ballochmyle in 1623. Charles Whitefoord of Blairquhan fought for the Hanoverians at the Battle of Culloden in 1746. Suffering disastrously from the effects of the Ayr Bank crash, in 1798 the family sold Blairquhan, together with an extensive estate of 14,000 acres, to the trustees of Sir David Hunter Blair and the castle remains under the ownership of this family today. This photograph shows the magnificent front view of the castle with a car parked outside the grand entrance with its lantern tower. Just off to the left was the flower garden and the lime avenue that led visitors up to the castle while on the right are the stable block, icehouse, garden pond and pinetum. Just out of view is the Dool (or Dule) Tree, a natural gallows for hanging criminals. Within the grounds was also a walled garden with a large glasshouse while the Water of Girvan flows behind the castle. The old castle that was dismantled stood on the ground just to the front of its successor. In 1970 the castle and grounds were first opened to the public for functions and special events and this continues to the present day.

This view of Kirkmichael from the west dates from July 1929. The Straiton Road is visible sweeping round to the right across the then new bridge over the Dyrock Burn and the playing fields where it would pass the entrance gates to Kirkmichael House just out of picture. The distinctive red sandstone McCosh Hall with its clock tower can be seen within the village on the Patna Road, while further along to the left, just visible above the trees, is the old chapel. On slightly raised ground near Clawbeg, to the right of the photograph, is the village school. Kirkmichael was once a thriving centre for the handloom weaving and many of the single-storey whitewashed cottages with their centre doors and offset twin windows for the loom shop line the streets.

Looking east along the Patna Road in July 1929. The *New Statistical Account* of 1838 stated that, 'The manufacture of cotton is the staple trade of the place. The large Glasgow warehouses appoint agents here, who give out the cotton to the handloom weavers, and are responsible for its manufacture into the required fabric. By this means, a large sum of money is transmitted weekly from Glasgow to the country. Children are put to the loom as early as the age of ten. Women are frequently as expert weavers as men. Women who have not been brought up to weave make a livelihood by filling bobbins. There is another very extensive branch of industry – the Ayrshire needlework, which is executed in this village in a very superior style. It is a valuable means of employment, and furnishes decent support to many respectable females, yet it is to be feared that the continual confinement, which is indispensable in order to subsistence will prove more injurious to health than if the work were harder, and the person more exposed.' The cottages seen here were among those where this industry was carried out.

Looking east along the Straiton Road in July 1929. The garage was owned by James Mirrey. Kirkmichael dates back to the 1200s when John de Gemmelstoun founded a small chapel, dedicated to St Michael, beside the Dyrock Burn. John was the son and heir of John de Gemilstoun, who was a knight, and the lands were confirmed to them by King James IV in 1451. The village started life as a small rural parish and was called Kirkmichael of Gemilstoun for many years. The present church dates from 1787 and stands at the locally named Kirkport, which has an attractive lich entrance gate dating back to 1702.

A group of visitors stand outside the entrance gates and gatehouse of Kirkmichael House in July 1929, when it was being used as a convalescent home for miners. At these entrance gates there were twelve old lime-trees known locally as the Twelve Apostles and one of these stands in the foreground. In the late seventeenth century the historian Abercrummie wrote, 'The house of Kirkmichael is a pretty commodious house, within a short space of the church of the same; betwixt which runs the water of the Dyrock . . . which soon swells with rains falling on the higher grounds, and becomes impassable on the sudden. The House of Kirkmichael is as desyreable a dwelling as in all the countrey, having good gardens and orchards; and was the first in Carrick planted with apricots and peaches. This orchard and house is flanked on the south with a loch; part whereof has been drained of late, and rewards the owner's industry with good hay.' Note the photographer's jacket hanging on the railings!

The sweeping drive up to the front entrance of Kirkmichael House, photographed in July 1929. A building was believed to have occupied this site as early as the fifteenth century and was built by Gilbert Kennedy, son of David Kennedy, sixth son of Sir Gilbert Kennedy of Dunure. In the seventeenth century a tower house was built by the Kennedy family and around 1830, when it was the property of Colonel Shaw Kennedy, this was incorporated into the present building to which a mock tower house was also later added in 1861. Kirkmichael House was substantially altered over the years with numerous additions but remained within the Kennedy family until 1920 when it was sold. The house was bought and converted into a miners' convalescent home and remained as such until 1956 when it was acquired by the local authority, painted bright pink and turned into a school for children with learning difficulties. It was used as a special needs school until 1992 when it was deemed no longer suitable for this purpose and was sold into private ownership in 1995.

Convalescing miners enjoy the tranquility and pleasant scenery on the banks of the large pond or 'The Loch', as it was known, at Kirkmichael House. James Paterson wrote in his *History of the County of Ayr* (1852) that, 'Kirkmichael House is an excellent and commodious family residence. There is still a lake in its vicinity – about five acres in extent – which adds greatly to the picturesque features of the situation. Vast improvements have been made on the grounds within these few years. There are some splendid trees within the policy, and very thriving plantations throughout the estate.' Today the house and gardens are being restored to their former magnificent condition.

'The Loch' is located to the rear of Kirkmichael House. The house remained under the ownership of the powerful Kennedy family for many generations until it was sold in 1920. An advert in *The Times* informed readers: 'Kirkmichael House, Maybole, Ayrshire, N.B., to be LET. Furnished, with a small moor and other shootings, rabbit warren, fishings, etc, for three or more years, as may be agreed upon, with immediate entry. The house contains accommodation for a large family; private gasometer and every convenience.'

Standing on a green knoll about a mile south of Maybole, Kilhenzie Castle dates from the late sixteenth century. The lands and castle were originally owned by the Kennedys of Bargany but later passed into the ownership of the Carrick branch of the Bairds who in the seventeenth century added a three-storey wing on to the tower. The Rev. William Abercrombie, writing in 1686, remarked that 'Many of the pretty dwellings of the gentry here are sweet desyrable places; but for the good building, gardens, orchards and all other accomodations, Kilhenzie is the chiefe, lying about a short myle south from the towne of Mayboll.' The feudal keep was in a ruinous condition by the 1850s when it became the property of Sir James Fergusson of Kilkerran, who restored it to its original condition. As can be seen in this photograph, by the early 1900s a small golf course had been created on the policies surrounding the castle.

Maybole viewed from the south, with the Ladywell Tannery and Boot Factory dominating the view. This was the largest factory in the town, established around 1870 by John Gray. It was later owned by the Miller Tanning Company Ltd, and employed only 45 people prior to its closure in May 1969. The brick chimney was once known as the 'Bog Lum'. Also visible in the background is the Town Hall and Tollbooth on Whitehall, while on the right are the chimneys of Lorne Boot and Shoe Factory and the factories at the Kirkwynd and St Cuthberts. In the foreground are Welltrees Square and the thatched cottages on the Dailly Road. This view has changed considerably with the building of modern housing in Miller Terrace, Hicks Avenue and at Ladywell.

An early 1900s view, looking southeast over Maybole from the Town Hall steeple. Dominating the view is the chimney of the Lorne Boot and Shoe Factory, owned at this time by John Lees and Co. It was the second largest factory in the town and at the time of this photograph employed 283 workers who produced on average 3,000 pairs of 'tackety' boots a week. John Lees and Co. also owned the Townend Boot and Shoe Factory. The Lorne factory had closed by 1950 due to large slump in the demand for leather boots as fashions changed. Just behind the factory was the town's gas works with the round gasometer just visible here while the Crosshill Road can be seen gently climbing past the new cemetery and onwards to the Lochbrae. The cemetery was opened in April 1851 and then enlarged in 1880 to occupy a site of two acres. To the left of the cemetery is the farm of Tunnoch.

The War Memorial Park in Maybole was created after the First World War when the residents purchased a large area of farmland at the south end of the town. A war memorial in the form of a large granite obelisk was erected at the highest spot in the park. On one sides of the memorial, inscribed in metal, are the 109 names from the First World War and the 30 names from the Second World War. The park was officially opened in 1925 when Maybole resident Mrs Clark, who had lost four sons during the First World War, unlocked the gates and was presented afterwards with a key-brooch to mark the occasion. The park contained a nine-hole golf course, tennis courts and a bowling green. In recent years the original metal gates disappeared - presumed stolen - after being removed for refurbishment by the council, although new gates in a similar style were dedicated at a special service in 2000. The public park now has a children's playground, tennis courts, a bowling green, a nine-hole golf course and even an indoor swimming pool.

The railway reached Maybole on 15 September 1856 when the line from Ayr was opened for goods traffic and then the following year, on 13 October, for passengers. The inhabitants of the town had petitioned for the service for many years and the town council even urged some local people to take out shares in this new venture. A small station was constructed at Redbrae and the line was known as the Ayr & Maybole Junction Railway. This station was later found to be unsuitable when the track was eventually extended all the way down the coast to Girvan by the Glasgow & South Western Railway Company. The present station, seen here, was opened in 1880. This view looks southwest along the double tracks towards the metal footbridge and then on to the road bridge at the Greenhead. On the right is the northbound platform with the signal box and the signalmen peering out towards the photographer while further along is the steeple of the Kincraig Church and the large single-storey waiting rooms with a glazed awning. On the left are the southbound platform and the distinctive two-storey red sandstone station building and ticket office. In 1973 the line became a single track and the northbound platform and waiting rooms were demolished. Much to the annoyance and anger of locals, in 2005 the old ornamental footbridge that had stood for 125 years was cut down and replaced with a ramp to allow disabled access across the track. A regular rail service still operates on the route.

A lone officer of the Ayrshire Constabulary keeps a watchful eye on the hundreds of factory workers heading home to enjoy their lunch before returning to complete their shift for the day. This view from 1902 is looking northwards from the Town Hall along High Street with the Castle visible in the distance, while cast on the street is the distinctive shadow from the town steeple and spooncreel. On the left of this view is the Dairy Corner and the narrow School Vennel that led to the Greenside while opposite is John Knox Street. This street was originally known as the Back Vennel but later became known as the Red Lion Brae after an inn that was located there. It was later changed to its present name to commemorate what is known locally as 'The Debate', which took place in a house there when John Knox met Quintin, Abbot of Crossraguel. A plaque now marks the site of this house.

THE CASTLE, MAYBOLE.    LATTA'S SERIES N° 316

Known locally simply as the 'Castle', Maybole Castle dates from the early seventeenth century and is an L-shaped tower of four storeys built in the traditional Scottish baronial style. It was commonly believed to have been built by Gilbert Kennedy, fifth Earl of Cassillis, who was the High Lord Treasurer of Scotland. It was described by the Rev. R. Lawson in his book *Views of Carrick* (1894) as being 'formerly the Town House of the Cassillis lords who ruled Carrick in days of old. Of recent years it has been considerably modernised; but the stout square keep in the centre has stood for considerably over 300 years. The pretty oriel window above lights the room where the Countess, who eloped with the gipsy laddie, is said to have been confined till the day of her death. The carved chimney heads, too, are much admired, as well as the quaintly ornamental windows.' The 'Castle' is the oldest inhabited building within Maybole and is used as the office for the management of the extensive Cassillis Estates.

Looking northwards along Maybole High Street towards the 'Castle' and into Cassillis Road, which was once known as New Yards. Tenant farmers living and working on the Earl of Cassillis's land often paid their rents in the form of crops and straw which was then duly carted to Maybole and stored in large granaries or stack yards which once existed near the castle. The spire of the parish church, dating from 1809, can be seen in the background.

The public green in Maybole was a large area of grass that had once been let annually by the town council for the grazing of livestock and it was also used by travelling shows for their marquees and entertainments during the summer at fairtime. In the 1850s it was known as the School Green as it had become the playground of local children attending the parish school, but in 1894 it was formerly laid out at a cost of £400, half the money being raised through public subscription. The green was levelled, planted with ornamental trees and railed in with formal paths running through it. In 1881 a memorial fountain built from Peterhead granite was erected over an old well to commemorate Thomas Dykes, factor to the Marquis of Ailsa and the first senior magistrate in the town council. He had lived within Maybole for forty years and the fountain was bequeathed by his daughter. On the left of this view is the row of houses known as Greenside, where the Greenside Inn was located, while at the top of the street the Kincraig Church, built in 1880, can be seen.

The Cairn School at Maybole was built in 1898 on an area known locally as the Kirklands. It had accommodation for 450 pupils and met the needs for primary education within the thriving town at this time. The Cairn School took its name from the grassy field on which it was built, where a cairn must have stood in times past to commemorate some long forgotten battle or incident. In recent years the school has been extensively modernised and still provides primary schooling for the town's children.

The Cargill United Free Church was built in 1844 in Barns Road and was named after the Covenanter, the Rev. Donald Cargill, who had preached near the town in May 1681. Cargill had been ousted from his ministerial duties at the Barony Church in Glasgow at the age of 71 and became a fugitive with a price of 5,000 merks on his head. He travelled to Maybole and held a large conventicle to the north of the town near Ladycross, where he preached from the top of a large whin boulder. Two months later he was apprehended by the authorities and hanged in Edinburgh and the boulder that was used as the pulpit was renamed Cargill's Stone in his memory. In 1843 the leaders of the local Free Church blasted the boulder with gunpowder and a large part of it was incorporated into the front wall of the Cargill Free Church. On 30 December 1906 the church was almost completely devastated by fire although it was later rebuilt by the congregation. In the 1950s, after nearby Kincraig Church had been sold to a local builder, its congregation combined with that of Cargill and it became known as the Cargill-Kincraig Church. The church was demolished in 1979 and modern houses have been built on the site with the name surviving in Cargill Court.

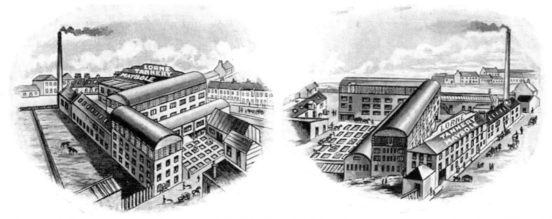

The Lorne Boot and Shoe Factory had been established by John Dick but the concern was purchased in 1875 by Mr Thomas A. Gray who expanded the tannery and modernised the works by installing electric lighting. By 1883 the works had become the second largest employer within the town, with 283 men and women producing on average 3,000 pairs of boots a week. Mr Gray also owned a large warehouse in Glasgow and a retail chain of over 30 shops but following a downturn in the industry he became bankrupt and in 1895 sold the tannery and factory to John Lees and Co. for a knockdown price (he later threw himself from a train into the River Clyde). John Lees also owned the Townend Boot and Shoe Factory near the Redbrae and in the early 1900s the works were in full production supplying rubberised boots to the Admiralty. Orders from the War Office ensured that the Lorne factory continued to provide employment during both world wars when the industry was in general decline. However, the factory was closed by the early 1950s and housing has since been built on the site.

The Townend Boot and Shoe Factory was founded in 1878 By John Lees, his son John, and also his son-in-law William McKellar. The large works were located on the Alloway Road near the Redbrae and overlooked the railway line and the railway station. There were originally only fifteen workers engaged in the manufacture of leather shoes and boots within an old wooden shed but the venture prospered and the firm moved into a purpose-built factory in the early 1890s to become one of the largest employers within the town. In 1895 John Lees also acquired the Lorne factory to ensure a reliable supply of tanned leather for the soles and heels and also finished leather for the uppers. By 1928 over 350 men and women were employed at the Townend works and there were also a large number of travellers or travelling salesmen who marketed and sold the finished boots and shoes around the globe. In June 1962 a terrible fire destroyed the factory and, as it was Maybole's main employer at the time, many locals became unemployed.

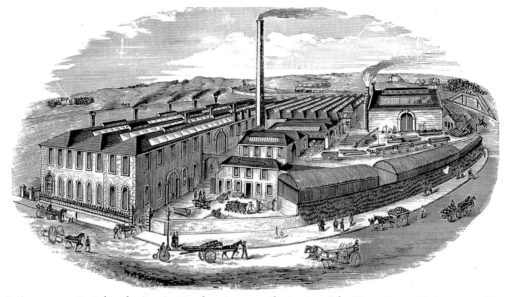

Mr Alexander Jack was a cartwright who lived at Auchendrane on the banks of the River Doon. He began making agricultural implements in 1840 and twelve years later purchased some land near the parish church at New Yards in Maybole, where he designed and built a modern works. These were powered by a large steam engine and had an engineering shop, blacksmith's shop, erecting (assembling) shop, foundry for the casting of iron and brass, a joiner's shop, a sawmill and well-stocked wood yards. The company manufactured potato raisers, mowers, reapers, manure distributors, all manner of carts, and an extensive range of ploughs and tools. It employed over 100 people and at its peak in the early years of the twentieth century the firm exhibited at agricultural shows across Britain, winning many silver and gold medals and trophies. Alexander's also became famed for its 'Oliver' ploughs and were also believed to have been the first to manufacture rubber-tyred cart wheels. The firm had initially manufactured horse-drawn implements but adapted with the times and its machine-drawn implements were often exported to places such as Australia and South Africa. When Mr Jack died in 1877, the business was continued on by his son-in-law John Marshall. The works closed in 1966.

Travelling from the Girvan Valley into Maybole the Coral Glen road passes through a small glen that was formerly an old stone quarry known as the 'Quarrie Glen' (in recent years corrupted into 'Coral Glen'). Located here is 'The Wee Spoot' or 'Cockydrighty' as it is known by locals. This was one of a number of wells or natural springs located within the town and was described by the Rev. R. Lawson in his book *Places of Interest about Maybole* (1891): 'Into this glen there has flowed, beyond the memory of man, a small spring of clear, cold water, which is known by the name of the Wee Spout. Fifty years ago, before the present road was formed, the Spout ran on the opposite side of the road, but when the road was made, its position was altered. About five years ago, the Wee Spout had fallen into such a ruinous state that it was of comparatively little use in summer, while it was a nuisance in winter, when the frozen water spread all over the road and made it dangerous for horses. By the help of a few public-spirited friends, however, the Wee Spout, at a cost of £32, was cleaned out and rebuilt, so that what was formerly a disgrace, is now an ornament.'

Shore Road was the main route out of the town that led to the sandy beaches along the shore at Croy and Culzean. This area was formerly known as the Gallow Hill and was the location of the town gallows. In the early twentieth century the street was renamed Culzean Road. Today the villas on the right still overlook the town but a new junction for modern housing at Queens Terrace and Kincraig Avenue has since been created at the position where the young girl is standing on the pavement.

The view looking southwards from Maybole towards Kildoon Hill. On the left are the isolated Ballony Tenements and garage, and next to them is the Ballony Farm, which was purchased by the town council for use as a sewage works and rubbish coup. On the right is the chimney of the Ladywell Tannery and Shoe Factory which closed in 1969. Beyond that is the spire of Our Lady and St Cuthbert's Church which was built from yellow and grey sandstone in 1878 on Allan's Hill. In the centre of this photograph is the Ladywell Stadium where the Maybole Juniors still play. On Kildoon Hill are the remains of a prehistoric fort and also a monument to a local landowner, Sir Charles Fergusson of Kilkerran, erected in 1853.

Cassillis Railway Station was located about a mile south from the small hamlet of Minishant on the Kirkmichael road; it was conveniently situated for the Kennedy house at Cassillis on the banks of the River Doon, after which it was named. The line was opened for goods traffic on 15 September 1856 and for passengers on 13 October 1857. The Glasgow & South Western Railway Company took it over in 1871 and Cassillis was initially no more than just a stop on the line until additional buildings and a stationmaster's house were added twenty years later. Cassillis Villa was also built nearby to cater for the large shooting parties who frequently arrived by train. Just a century after the first trains had stopped at Cassillis the small station closed in 1956 and the last stationmaster, James Blackwood, bought the station house and lived there during his retirement.